Practical Liquidity Management

Practical Liquidity Management

A Means to Financial Strength in Companies

MICHAEL TENNENT, FCA

Gower Press

First published in Great Britain by Bowker Publishing Company Limited, Epping, Essex, 1976

Gower Press is an imprint of Bowker Publishing Company Limited

ISBN 0 7161 0326 5

Set in Times 10 on 12 point

Printed in Great Britain
at the University Printing House, Cambridge
(Euan Phillips, University Printer)

Contents

Illustrations

Foreword

by Kenneth F. Dibben, BCom, FCA, Director, Hambros Bank Limited

It used to be said: The name of the game is profit. Every company coming to the City knew that its profit record and profit projections would be crucial to any financing proposition. If the private sector is to have a future this must remain true. Nevertheless, the lesson of the recent past is that profit is not enough — there is a second, equally necessary, game which must be played in parallel: its name is survival and its prerequisite liquidity.

Every banker's apprentice is taught that to borrow short and lend long is a certain recipe for ruin but he quickly learns also that such a situation is inherent in banking! Indeed, a case can be made for saying that the old adage conceals a more significant lesson because it concentrates attention on too narrow an aspect of cash management. The greater truth is that insolvency is the inability to meet liabilities as they fall due and it is characterised not, as many suppose, by an absence or inadequacy of assets but by their wrong disposition within the business.

In this book the author shows that in the management of business liquidity every entry on the balance sheet — left or right, top or bottom — has a contribution to make and that every decision of management, at whatever level, affects the ultimate balance of liquidity.

The techniques, as well as the principles, of cash management are exhaustively described, and the author puts under revealing scrutiny many long-accepted management ratios, now due for critical review.

This book is commended to finance directors and company treasurers and all those who seek an understanding of financial management. It can be read at many levels: undoubtedly it will establish its place in the literature of management for it meets a need not readily fulfilled elsewhere.

Acknowledgements

I should like to thank most sincerely the directors and executives of Gower Press who inspired me to write this book and upon whose advice I drew so liberally during the all-important initial stages of 'structuring' the work, and my wife, who 'went back to typing' and zealously wrestled with my hurried hieroglyphics.

I should also like to thank the many companies whose finances I have reviewed and restructured and whose financial problems have each presented me with a different and interesting challenge, and the equally many banks and other financial institutions with whom I have negotiated funds for clients; collectively, they have provided the backbone to my practical experience upon which this work is based.

Dedication

To the many company directors whose days appear largely to consist of grappling with the complexities and the unintelligibility of an ever-increasing proliferation of statutory dictates — businessmen who strive to utilise their days productively, but who find their initiatives stifled at almost every turn by impracticable and unsympathetic form-filling governmental bureaucrats — 'little-minded' men who demand licences to do this and permits to do that, who levy taxes on this and duties on that, and who appear impelled to drain away the last vestiges of individuality which once made ours the greatest trading nation on earth.

May an efficient system of liquidity management in these directors' companies at least enable them to maximise the use of their unconfiscated capital, to minimise the risk of being overtaken by a cash crisis and, as a result, to relax more beneficially when at last each frustrating day is done.

Part 1

Introduction

Whether your business is in manufacturing, wholesaling or retailing, heavy industry or light, goods or services or whatever, it has at least one need in common with every other business — cash.

Indeed, this is the commodity dealt in more than any other by your business — and everyone else's. In the light of this undeniable fact, it is surprising that in so many companies so small a proportion of the time is devoted to planning and generally looking after this unique and indispensable commodity.

(From an article by the Author, which appeared in *European Industrial and Commercial Review* in 1975.)

1

The challenge of inflation

High inflation is a challenge to test the mettle of the most experienced boards of directors and, in many more companies than are willing to admit the fact, liquidity problems are approaching danger level. Probably there is an even greater number of companies which do not know whether they have a problem or not — but almost certainly do.

Unquestionably these problems are going to sort out, in the years if not months ahead, those companies which know where they are and where they are going from those which, knowingly or unknowingly, are being carried towards the rocks by the irrepressible force of the financial current.

Every company is different and needs thinking about differently, but it is an irresponsible management on this tightrope which rejects the simplest of liquidity management techniques, thereby dismissing at least the chance to remove its blindfold in order to see which way it is facing and where the nearest refuge is offered.

Insuring against 'illiquidity'

Only a fool delays paying the premium on his fire insurance policy, believing the time to do this is when the smoke is first spotted coming up between the floorboards. The same fool would, no doubt, say a year's premium was a waste of money if no claim were made before it expired.

To *plan* a company's liquidity is to 'insure' against an unexpected crisis. It is a premium well worth paying in times when business crashes are running at their highest level since the war.

But liquidity management, however sophisticated, will not produce miracles, nor will it guarantee wisdom to boards which lack the basic capacity to manage in a rapidly changing, and daily more challenging, environment. Liquidity management is not going to save a company which is already over the edge; it is not, by itself, going to make it possible to avoid an overtrading situation for a company which is inherently undercapitalised.

Liquidity management will make the most of a company's resources, highlight the weak financial spots and signal the areas where remedial action will be most effective. It will be found beneficial to all companies, large and small.

Need to be properly informed

Underlying the advice given in almost every section of this book is the need for management to be properly informed and many positive proposals to achieve this end are included. Too many boards of directors find themselves submerged beneath voluminous reports and statistics which, if they are not useless because they are either inappropriate or circulated too late to be acted upon, require a sleuth to find the key factors and an accomplished linguist to make these intelligible to the everyday business manager.

This book, it is hoped, will demonstrate that liquidity management is not technical mumbo-jumbo intelligible only to academics, but a practical means by which the chances of the very survival of *every* business — large and small — can be materially improved. The methods described in this book stem from common sense and experience, and have been largely developed during the practical work of the author while acting as either financial consultant or financial director to a wide range of companies and groups, and in his own businesses as a successful entrepreneur.

To operate liquidity management — as described in this book — boards of directors will be required to plan in detail in order to determine where their companies are going and, again, to plan in detail in order to ensure they have the resources to get them there.

A banker was recently overheard making what amounted to a terrifying condemnation of the current financial stability of British business. He said: 'We only lend to half our customers, because if we did not, the other half would be put out of business!' How more tenuous can one get?

Inflationary constraints

Finance — the most limiting factor

What is referred to when the 'size' of a company is talked about? Is it the number of staff employed, the extent of its property interests, the level of capital employed or profits earned, or what? Most people would say that in the context of business, 'size' is generally taken to be a reflection of the level of turnover.

The turnover in most companies is determined by a combination of:

1 The market potential — the level of customer demand the salesmen could satisfy
2 The physical capacity — the level of output the company's factories could manufacture, could store and could distribute
3 The management capacity — the size of undertaking the board and middle management have the ability to develop and control effectively
4 The finance available — the level necessary to maintain adequate working capital and to replace fixed assets when needed, and to expand

In most businesses today, it is the finance which is the most limiting factor, and the great majority of companies which get into liquidity difficulties do so because they overlooked the restraints of their financial capacity.

In those idyllic days, when the meaning of the word 'inflation' was unknown to housewives and most company directors, the final measure of success in business was always 'profit'. In these inflationary days, the prime test must be on two counts: profit *and* liquidity for, to go for profit at the expense of liquidity is to court disaster in a highly inflationary and generally unsympathetic business environment.

The purchasing power of cash flow

In conditions of no inflation, one year's results can be compared directly with another's and, likewise, the cash-flow retention from one year can, since it has a constant purchasing power, be utilised in subsequent periods either to buy the same quantity of raw materials and other goods for resale (and meet expense costs) or to replace worn-out fixed assets with identical units.

In conditions of inflation, and more so in times of an increasing rate of inflation, there is a constant diminution in the purchasing power of cash. Thus, the cash flow revealed in a company's accounts (calculated on an historical monetary basis) will not be capable of acquiring its full current face value's worth of goods the following year. To avoid such erosion in value, all financial surpluses accruing should be utilised at once, but this is often not as simple as it may sound.

The street-corner newspaper vendor, who buys, say, £10 of evening papers and sells them the same day for £15 is earning a gross profit of 33⅓ per cent. If the next week there is an all-round increase in prices of 10 per cent he will pay £11 for the same quantity of papers and sell them for £16.50 — still making a 33⅓ per cent gross profit. In arithmetical terms, therefore, inflation has not adversely affected the real value of his cash flow.

But the manufacturing company, which may buy its raw materials and work on them (adding labour costs and overheads in the process) over a period of months, passing the items eventually into its finished-goods stock from whence they become distributed to customers and paid for several months later, can be drastically affected by the drop in the purchasing power of its cash flow over the intervening period.

Why companies find themselves 'short'

One of the most common causes of all business failures is the lack of a sufficient capital base (long-term borrowings as well as share capital).

This arises, more often than not, from neglect to establish in advance what the company's financial requirements are and to plan its operations accordingly. Inflationary conditions have accentuated this need to quantify these requirements well in advance.

Most oversights of this nature arise from the failure to recognise that working capital can all too quickly, and permanently, render immobile very substantial and increasing proportions of a company's overall capital.

Rolls-Royce came to grief largely because the company failed to do its sums correctly on liquidity, and tied up too large a portion of its available capital in work-in-progress on the RB 211.

Under conditions of high inflation more cash is required to finance a business's existing volume of turnover even with no physical increase at all (what is referred to as 'Just maintaining the turnover in real terms').

The summarised accounts of a small manufacturing company shown in Figures 1:1 and 1:2 afford an illustration of (*a*) the effects inflation can have on the requirement for working capital and (*b*) how misleading, at first sight, ordinary financial accounts can be in judging the sufficiency of cash flow.

Figure 1:1 Trading and profit and loss account

	£'000
Sales	(1000)
Cost of sales	660
Gross profit	(340)
Expenses	150
Depreciation	30
Net profit before tax	(160)
Taxation	80
Net profit after tax	(80)
Dividends	40
Retained Earnings	(40)
Cash flow*	(70)

*Assuming the tax liability actually paid in the year equalled the charge in the current year's accounts.

Figure 1:2 Balance sheet extract (mid-point of year*)

	£'000
Stocks	165 (a)
Trade debtors	250 (b)
	415
Trade creditors	110 (c)
Working capital	305 (d)

*The average of the balance-sheet figures at the beginning and end of the financial year may be taken in companies without a strong seasonal pattern to their trade.

(a) 3 months (4 times turned over per annum)
(b) 3 months sales
(c) 3 months raw materials — 2 months on overall cost of sales
(d) Cash at bank, current tax liability and other net current asset items are assumed, in this simple example, to cancel each other out

Effects of inflation

If inflation is running at, say, 2 per cent per month (26.8 per cent a year), then subject to any change in the tax liability and long-term capital structure of the company, the working capital of £305,000 would be expected to reach about £387,000 in a further year's time (an increase in monetary terms of £82,000) in order merely to maintain the existing volume of turnover.

But the cash flow (calculated on a historical purchasing power basis) is only £70,000 and the chances are that at least some of the fixed assets of the company would be due for replacement, and would have to be paid for out of this sum. Depreciation is only £30,000. It is rare today to find that the depreciation retention of cash, which is also calculated on a historical cost basis, provides more than a small fraction of the funds which are necessary to replace manufacturing assets bought perhaps 20 years previously.

But the deception is even more fundamental. What the accounts fail to make allowance for is that the unit of £s used to quantify the sales are not of the same value as the £s used to describe purchases and costs. Because of inflation there has been a change in purchasing power and, therefore, 'value' between the time the purchases were made and the time the goods made from them were sold. In 'real terms', therefore, the profit is overstated.

The subject of 'current cost accounting' is both topical and far-reaching. Readers will find that many of the principles involved have a direct relevance to liquidity management and the constant up-dating of the purchasing power of company 'retentions'.

Inflation and the 'settlement time-lag'

Whatever the rate of inflation, in the great majority of businesses there is a time-lag to be allowed for during which the purchasing power of earnings is diminished. This is often overlooked in liquidity planning, but as the illustrations below demonstrate all too clearly, the 'book profit' earned at the time of a sale is of an altogether different value to the cash increment which is realised later. This inescapable further call upon financial resources must be allowed for.

If the example described in Figures 1:1 and 1:2 is analysed, this diminution in purchasing power and what it means in terms of the cash flow can be quantified.

It is, perhaps, easiest to follow this analysis if one transaction, being typical of the company and leading to a sale of goods for £100, is examined step by step. For the first stage in this examination, the credit given by the suppliers and the credit given to the customers is ignored. It will be seen from Figure 1:2 that the stock investment of £66 is held over an average period of three months. The financial accounts, which ignore time as such, would reflect this transaction simply as:

Sale	£100.00
Cost of sale	66.00
Gross profit	£ 34.00

Replacement cost

But the cost of the sale and the sale itself are not both expressed in units of the same purchasing power. The cost of replacing the £66 of stock at the time the sale was made would, at the assumed 2 per cent per month rate of inflation for three months, involve expenditure of £70.04 — on this basis, the 'real profit' would have been only £29.96.

However, the above example is not one involving a cash sale and a repurchase of stock for spot cash. The company allowed the customer three months' credit, during which time the purchasing power of the £100 selling price would have fallen to £94.23.

Similarly, the suppliers allowed three months' credit on raw materials such that, after taking into account other manufacturng costs, an average of two months' credit would have been gained on the replacement 'cost of sale' figure of £70.04; the two months' drop in purchasing power would have lowered this 'cost' to £67.32.

Figure 1:3 Gross profit comparisons due to inflation and the time-lag

	(1) Financial accounts	(2)* Accounts in 'real terms'	(3) Cash flow in 'real terms'
Sale	£100.00	£100.00	£94.23
Cost of sale	66.00	70.04	67.32
Gross profit/ trading cash flow	£ 34.00	£ 29.96	£26.91
Difference with financial accounts:		£4.04	£7.09

*Replacement-cost basis

These facts are all put together in Figure 1:3 which shows that at the 'gross profit' level, in 'real terms' the profit from this sale would be worth £4.04 less, and the final cash increment, when received, £7.09 less, than what the conventional form of accounts would show, both reductions being on account of inflation and its effect on the purchasing power of cash. These 'losses' represent in this example approximately 4 and 7 per cent, respectively, of the selling price — approximately 12 and 21 per cent of the gross profit stated.

Although the example given is of a single sale, it is one of very many such sales, the total of which constitutes the whole trading pattern of the finances upon which the company exists.

'Real terms' cash flow

What else is significant about these three different expressions of the same transaction?

1 Financial accounts — this is the manner in which the shareholders will see the transaction reflected and the one on which (at the net-profit level) the public's calculation of the company's cash flow will be based — cash flow, that is, in purely monetary terms. It is also upon the resulting net profit that the Revenue will base their tax assessments.
2 Accounts in 'real terms' — the real financial profit from the transaction was only £29.96 and provided the company intends to continue trading and its credit standing with bankers and suppliers is such that it does not have to await the actual receipt of cash before it can commence to recycle the same funds, this is the figure which, after deduction of other costs, reveals the flow of funds (in this instance 'credit'), which is available, for example, to purchase replacement plant or new equipment for the growth of the company.
3 Cash flow in 'real terms' — the real purchasing power of the actual cash gain resulting from the profit yielded. This is the significant figure if the company is, as so many companies are today, at the limit of its borrowing resources — eg its bankers have put an absolute limit on its overdraft as a result of which purchases of new plant and even replacement stock literally depend on the speed with which cash can be collected from debtors. During the time-lag of collection, of course, prices continue to rise and the cash, when eventually it is received, will be found to purchase less. It is not uncommon to find

suppliers to such companies placing restrictive limits on the credit allowed so that (*a*) raw materials have to be bought in smaller, and more costly, quantities and (*b*) essential deliveries are held up pending the settlement of earlier months' supplies. Cash rather than credit becomes the operative factor in these situations, hence the relevance of the significant 'loss' between the results of columns (1) and (3), in Figure 1:3.

Net cash flow

So far, only the 'real-terms' cash flow at the gross-profit level has been considered. However, what affects a company's ability to replace assets, to finance new assets in order to expand etc., is the net cash flow — the final surplus which largely stems from the sum of (*a*) retained profits (i.e. after tax and dividends have been met) and (*b*) depreciation. There is invariably credit to be gained on a company's tax liabilities and generally on both its overhead costs and dividend payments. Accordingly, it is usual to find at least a part of the 'loss' described in Figure 1:3 being recovered, in cash-flow terms, at the net-profit level.

Inflationary effects on seasonal companies

The previous example concerned a manufacturing company with a non-seasonal trade and in which, on average, stock was turned over a fairly typical four times each year.

There are many companies which operate in seasonal markets with some (for example, manufacturers of fireworks, crackers, calendars and diaries) whose annual selling season is very short. There are, too, other types of companies whose manufacturing cycles extend over more than 12 months. For these companies, the time-lag is very long and, relatively, more costly in terms of lost value in their cash flow.

Take, for example, a company with the same trading accounts as those summarised in Figure 1:1, whose factory is in production the whole year but whose selling is concentrated into, say, three months. The effects of inflation during the time-lags of such a company become very marked as is evident from the following summarised particulars:

Months 1 to 12 (average end of month 6)

Purchases: £660,000 (4½ months ahead of the mean date, see below, when the sales are made, by which time the replacement cost would be £722,000)

Months 3 to 14 (average end of month 8)

Payment to suppliers: £660,000 (by which time the purchasing power of the cash paid out on a replacement-cost basis would have dropped from £722,000 to £694,000

Months 10 to 12 (average month 11)

Goods sold for £1,000,000

Months 13 to 15 (average month 14)

Receive £1,000,000 cash (by which time the real value has dropped, as compared with month 11, to £942,000)

A comparison in gross-profit terms of a single sale of goods priced at £100 for this company reveals the figures shown in Figure 1:4.

Figure 1:4 Gross profit comparisons due to inflation and the time-lag (seasonal manufacturer)

	(1) Financial accounts	(2) Accounts in 'real terms'	(3) Cash flow in 'real terms'
Sale	£100.00	£100.00	£94.23
Cost of sale	66.00	72.15	69.35
Gross profit/ trading cash flow	£ 34.00	£ 27.85	£24.88
Difference with financial accounts		£ 6.15	£ 9.12

Apparent and real results

For such a company, therefore, the combination of inflation and time-lag would cost it, as compared with what the conventional form of accounts would show, approximately 6 and 9 per cent of the selling price, and approximately 18 and 27 per cent of the gross profit depending upon whether column (2) or (3) of Figure 1:4 was relevant. As in the previous example, at the net-profit level, some of the apparently 'lost' cash flow would be recovered through deferred payment of taxation etc.

However, for this seasonal company what is more relevant than the average position (shown in the first column of Figure 1:5) are the peaks in working-capital requirements, which generally have to be financed by means of short-term borrowings. Hence, in this simple example, the likely position at the end of month 9 (immediately before the selling season begins) and month 12 (immediately after it has finished, but before the cash from it has been received) are also shown.

Figure 1:5 Balance sheet extracts (seasonal manufacturer)

	Average for year £'000	End of month 9 £'000	End of month 12 £'000
Stocks:			
Normal level (from Figure 1:2)	165	175	186
Seasonal increment in finished goods	237	480	—
	402	655	186
Trade debtors	250	—	1000
	652	655	1186
Trade creditors	110	117	124
Working capital (excluding other net current asset items)	542	538	1062

It should be noted that the mere invoicing and delivery of goods, which gives rise to balance-sheet changes (goods at cost price, which have been included in stock, become debtors at selling price), does not of itself call for any immediate increase in financial resources. Thus, in the third column of Figure 1:5, the total of £1,062,000 is, in cash-requirement terms, overstated by £340,000 (representing the gross profit which has yet to be realised in cash on selling £660,000 of goods).

However, in the seasonal example above, there is another factor to be allowed for. The overhead expenses, which during the whole 12 months of the year will not be covered by realised cash profits (as was the case, month by month, in the non-seasonal company), will need to be funded; these could add a sizeable figure to the peak borrowing requirements.

Inflationary effects on peak borrowings

In the case of seasonally orientated companies (and few companies are wholly non-seasonal), the calculation of the working-capital requirement must be based on the peak. Taking inflation at 2 per cent per month, as before, working-capital requirements of the example seasonal company would be expected to increase as shown in Figure 1:6.

Figure 1:6 Working-capital requirements (seasonal manufacturer)

	Year 0 £'000	Year 1 £'000	Amount of increase £'000
Average	542	687	145
End of month 9	538	682	144
End of month 12	1062	1347	285

When these additional working-capital requirements are compared with the net after-tax results which are likely to flow from a company with a year's gross profit of only £340,000 (it should not be overlooked that no allowance has yet been made for the almost certain need to finance the replacement of fixed assets), it can be seen why this example company is likely to find itself 'short'.

What, in practice, is more relevant to seasonal companies is the fact that banks, which have generally been the source for financing seasonal build-ups of stock, are becoming more loath to increase authorised 'maximum facilities' (albeit that they may only be required for a few months of a year) on a scale which matches the short-term demands of inflation. Agreeing to increase just the 'average facility' of a company is of little practical use in funding the peaks.

The vicious circle

It is the creditors which usually suffer — companies which may themselves be experiencing cash crises — so that a vicious circle is begun, or more likely enlarged, and inflation continues its cancerous course through scores of interrelated businesses, large and small.

Such is the lot of almost all companies in these difficult inflationary conditions, but the boards of seasonally orientated businesses, as the example above serves to illustrate, undoubtedly have an extra dimension to the financial problems with which they daily have to grapple.

Readers are advised to work out the 'real' cash flow of their own companies on the lines described above. In most cases, the result will be found to provide a fairly conclusive answer to the question so often posed: Why, when we are making reasonable profits, do we always seem to be short of cash?

The inflationary ratio

The strain on cash resources, in order to finance working capital in times of inflation, has been demonstrated earlier in this chapter.

The three headings included in working capital, which are each directly affected (though not necessarily to the same extent) by inflation (in monetary terms), are stock, debtors and credtitors.

The current tax liability, dividends and the bank position also, obviously, reflect inflationary influences on the company's trading, but these items can be, and usually are, also affected by other considerations.

The ratio found by the following formula will tend to increase under inflationary conditions unless positive steps are taken either to inject more long-term borrowings into a business or to increase its cash-flow retentions:

$$\frac{\text{Stock} + \text{debtors} - \text{creditors}}{\text{capital employed}}$$

Provided this ratio is considered, not in isolation, but with the 'essential ratios' (see Chapter 13), it can provide a further useful insight into the course a company's liquidity standing is taking.

Anti-profit legislation

To add to the complexity of problems encompassing the vexed businessman, successive governments have enacted price codes and the like which, with all too great effect, have thrown nooses around the necks of companies trying to make, not just profits (why is this such a dirty word to most politicians?), but retained earnings — cash flow. As has been shown in this chapter, such retained profits are essential in times of high inflation to make up for the eroded purchasing power of the capital base of companies if not, also, to provide the means for expansion and the general flourishing of the nation's trade.

A motorist, driving a car round a corner, is suddenly confronted with the choice of (*a*) running over a child who has fallen off his bicycle or (*b*) crossing the double white line against the law — which alternative should he choose? Many company managements are facing similar choices today, when to constrain their profit level within the letter of the law is to take their company one step nearer to being run over by the uncaring momentum of inflation.

This book should not be used as a platform for political preaching, but pragmatic businessmen are aware that to limit profits for any significant length of time is to limit cash flow and, thereby, to thwart companies' chances of keeping pace with inflation. The ultimate end can only be the demise of their companies, the end of the private sector and a total surrender to universal state ownership.

By way of concluding this introductory chapter, all that can be said in favour of such a state of affairs, when and if it is reached, is that businessmen would have no further need for this book. Liquidity management for every corporate entity would be in the sole hands of the Chancellor of the Exchequer!

2

The need to plan

The importance of financial management

In large groups of companies there is often to be found a treasurer as well as a financial director, and both will be supported by highly qualified staff such that, financially, it can be claimed in so far as manning is concerned, 'everything is under control'.

Alas, in all too many medium-sized and smaller groups of companies there exists no more than a single director or controller to carry the whole financial brief. Sometimes the incumbent will shoulder many other responsibilities as well. The pressures on his working hours may well be such that little time is spent on the financial discipline (non-financial directors and managers so often believe that the 'figure work' just happens anyway and needs little directing as such).

If the reader is still in doubt, let it be stated without qualification that in *every* company, however large or small, the financial management is as important a job as any. And the manpower responsible must be allowed the time to plan and act effectively.

Involving the financial staff

The financial staff must never be downgraded to the level of glorified book-keepers. With the right calibre of staff, the financial section can, even if only as avoiders of unnecessary costs and losses, become one of the best profit-generating divisions in a company. They should be involved by every other department of management in everything they are planning and doing.

For example, the cost accountant should not be confined, as he is so often, to the factory. He should be given rein (with specific briefs and follow-up) in the sales division, in the purchasing section, in the despatch and every other profit centre and cost centre where evaluating prices, costs and methods is consciously or unconsciously a part of the everyday operation.

More often than not, the management of funds in the small and medium-sized business is more critical than in the large enterprise. Smaller companies do not have the same flexibility that large corporations have; the smaller company has not the same standing, the same 'creditworthiness' and finds, pro rata, bank and other loans less easily obtainable.

The need in every company, large and small, is for positive financial management. In times of high inflation and a generally tight credit policy nationally, more companies than are prepared to acknowledge the fact are faced with a straight choice: liquidity management now or probable cash crisis later.

One often hears company directors claiming to be 'very worried' about their overdraft. It could be said, in reply, that directors are paid to worry. Be that as it may, the simple message of this book is that their time should not be passed in worrying about the overdraft, but about whether every possible step is being taken by their company so as not to have to worry about the overdraft. This is not just a play on words, but an irrefutable claim than an efficient and carefully planned system of liquidity management will largely enable the overdraft to look after itself.

The probable inadequacy of cash flow

The effective worth of cash flow was compared in Chapter 1 with the figures appearing in a company's financial accounts.

Under conditions of high rates of inflation, it is too much to expect cash flow to cover the majority of companies' 'every need'. But what exactly has the annual cash-flow sum to meet in terms of future expenditure if recourse to new funds from outside of the company is to be avoided?

1 *Under conditions of 'no growth'* (ie maintenance of the same volume of sales in physical terms):
   (*a*) Working capital — the inflationary uplift in prices (over 12 months) between, basically, (i) raw materials, work-in-progress, finished stocks and debtors on the one hand, and (ii) trade creditors on the other.
   (*b*) Fixed-asset replacements — the inflationary uplift in prices (generally over many years) between (i) the cost of each new

replacement asset and (ii) the sale price of the old items plus the cash equivalent of the depreciation charged in earlier years' accounts (this latter charge will have been based on historical cost, perhaps 10 or 20 years previously). Furthermore, unless a sum of cash equivalent to these depreciation charges has actually been put aside for the purpose each year (and such prudence is rarely found these days) this 'depreciation retention' will not be available in ready cash. Hence, for all practical purposes, cash flow must be looked upon to fund the whole cost of the replacements less only any cash realised on the sale of the items replaced (often only of scrap value).

2 *Under conditions of 'planned expansion'* (extra calls upon cash flow to those listed under (1)):
   (*a*) Working capital — the 'real cost' plus the inflationary uplift in prices (over the period since the point in time used as the basis for such 'real costs').
   (*b*) Additional fixed assets — the total 'real cost' plus the inflationary uplift, as above.

Against a background of soaring costs working capital, as has been seen above, must have first call upon what funds are available. And there cannot be many companies which are sufficiently profitable to be in a position to plan a worthwhile expansion of business without having first to seek new capital.

Industrial investment

Successive governments seem to have been surprised at the low level of industrial investment in new plant and machinery — and this despite favourable grants and tax allowances. The simple truth is that industry today, particularly with pricing restraints on its own output, is just not generating sufficient cash flow and, in all probability, cannot afford to borrow all the finance that it would otherwise like to for any but the bare essentials of capital outlay.

The cost of borrowing, and generally also the cost of redeeming such borrowings, becomes another call upon the already inadequate cash flow.

Thus the almost inevitable shortfall in the self-generated capital base of a company during periods of high inflation, does highlight the importance of management quantifying accurately what amounts to the company's unavoidable extra financial needs. The directors should then arrange for the preparation of a comprehensive case (see Chapter 4), justifying the extra requirement, and for this to be ready for presentation to the relevant parties well in advance of any cash shortage becoming critical.

Return on capital employed

The underlying objective of all companies must be long-term prosperity. Amongst other considerations, this calls for the maximising of the return on the capital employed since, in turn, this is generally a prerequisite for growth in earnings per share (a statistic now required to be given in published accounts) which, in turn, is necessary in order to secure long-term shareholder support. (Keeping the shareholders sweet is a requirement not to be overlooked in financial planning.)

But the return on capital employed and the earnings per share do not move in precise correlation with one another. For example, the former takes no account of gearing or of the tax on profits. Earnings per share, on the other hand, is based on the after-tax (and after-interest) distributable surplus and would, therefore, be directly affected by a change in either long-term debt or the rate of corporation tax.

The desired improvement in the return on capital employed, as in most other aspects of finance, will only be achieved by detailed planning and monitoring. The return must, therefore, feature at the planning stages and not be ignored until it appears as an actual result in the historical accounts of the company.

Figure 2:1 Earnings per share

	Year 1 £'000	No extra debt Year 2(A) £'000	With extra debt Year 2(B) £'000
Trading profit	250	258	500
Loan-stock interest	50	50	100
Net profit before tax	200	208	400
Taxation at 50%	100	104	200
Earnings (profits available for appropriation)	100	104	200
Dividends	40		
Retained profits	60		

	£'000	£'000	£'000
Share capital (1,000,000 £1 ordinary shares)	1,000	1,000	1,000
Reserves (opening balance)	200	260	260
EQUITY INTEREST	1,200	1,260	1,260
10% loan stock	500	500	1,000
Deferred tax etc.	300	300	300
CAPITAL EMPLOYED	2,000	2,060	2,560
Gearing	(42%)	(40%)	(79%)
Earnings per share:			
Year 1: $\frac{£100,000}{1,000,000}$	10.0p		
Year 2A: $\frac{£104,000}{1,000,000}$		10.4p	
Year 2B: $\frac{£200,000}{1,000,000}$			20.0p
Return on capital employed:			
Year 1: $\frac{£250,000}{£2,000,000}$	12.5%		
Year 2A: $\frac{£258,000}{£2,060,000}$		12.5%*	
Year 2B: $\frac{£500,000}{£2,560,000}$			19.5%

*In this example, trading profits have increased over year 1 by exactly the proportion in which the previous year's retained profits (£60,000) augmented the total capital employed, thus the return remains constant. But note that the earnings per share have improved, though by less than the shareholders were entitled to expect (the increase is 4 per cent, whereas they ploughed back into the business before year 2 £60,000 which increased their equity interest by 5 per cent).

The maintenance of an acceptable return on capital employed is a function of a company's capital structure. Furthermore, if thought is being given to raising additional permanent capital, consideration should be given to the tax advantages (as well as to the effects on the returns which will be achieved) that can accrue from introducing a 'part-debt' structure on the lines illustrated in Figure 3:4.

For this purpose, it is relevant to consider an illustration comparing the return on capital employed with earnings per share (Figure 2:1).

For certain other and not infrequently used 'returns', the following adjustments are necessary:

1 Return on net worth — calculate this on the after-interest (pre-tax) profits
2 Return on equity interest — if there are preference shares, the total net dividend payable on them should be grossed up at the corporation tax rate (not the income tax rate) and deducted from the pre-tax profits in order to arrive at the proportion of pre-tax profits which, subject only to tax, are wholly at the disposal of the equity shareholders. (If there are no preference shares, the return on equity interest is the same as on net worth.)

The financial requirement in marketing

Too many companies regard marketing as just a 'selling operation' — an activity which, basically, needs only to be planned in collaboration with the production wing of the same company. All the brainpower of companies, it would seem, is brought to bear on appraisals of new capital purchases. What so few directors appear to realise is that the marketing plan is every bit as dependent upon finance as the purchase of a new piece of expensive plant.

Marketing represents an investment in resources — in working capital — and in times of inflation this calls for an ever-increasing investment in terms of retained earnings merely to maintain turnover at the same level in 'real terms'.

Therefore, if companies are not to find themselves running out of financial capacity ('overtrading'), whether new products and new markets are being planned or not, the whole marketing plan requires detailed financial appraisal on a par with any other form of investment. The method for evaluating this will be dealt with later.

It must already be clear that retained earnings play an important role in the ability of a company to keep its head above the inflationary waters which surround it. Apart from introducing new capital, a simple formula emerges:

retentions less cost of asset replacements
= financial capacity to increase turnover

(in this context, turnover is in monetary terms, not 'real terms').

Retentions are dependent upon profits which, without due consideration, too many companies directly relate to turnover. To increase turnover 'at all costs' seems to be the mistaken message emerging from all too many boardrooms. The need to limit turnover will be considered in depth later, but many diectors may become convinced that to decrease their turnover will not only be better for liquidity, but also for their profits in today's strange financial climate.

The financial requirement for taxation

The apparent benevolence of the Revenue in allowing companies from 9 to 23 months (the exact period depends upon the date they used to pay their Schedule D tax) from the end of their financial year in which to pay their corporation tax, can be, and very often is, the final straw for a company which meets an unexpected, albeit temporary, lowering of its profits. Few companies are sufficiently strong in cash terms today to buy tax certificates or otherwise to earmark specific funds to meet future tax demands; the great majority are glad of the use of such funds right up to the very last of the days of grace allowed in order to help augment their overstretched resources.

Taxation on the previous year's profits has still to be paid and the bill will hit a company hardest in the first year that its profits (and, hence, its current cash flow) fails to maintain the level of earlier years. For taxation purposes, subsequent years' losses can enable a company to reclaim some of the tax it has paid in recent years (including advance corporation tax), but such is the time-lag (while accounts are prepared, delivered to and accepted by the Revenue) that very often the Inland Revenue's refund reaches the company after it has otherwise exhausted its financial resources and the shutters are already up.

The outside adviser

Many groups of companies, including some of the giants of industry, employ financial advisers on either an ad hoc or regular basis. These specialists in high finance cannot relieve the directors of any of their personal obligations to the company, but they do provide a useful function. This is particularly so when funds have to be raised, for such specialists generally have close and useful associations in the City.

Moving down the size scale of companies, it is not uncommon to find the auditors playing an advisory role, but usually only when consulted on specific subjects.

Further down the scale still, one finds many small company managements who look upon their auditors almost as one of themselves with shared responsibilites. This is, of course, a myth and one it is important to eradicate.

The same professional firm of accountants, even the same partners and staff, may visit a company wearing more than one hat. The same people may, for example, deal with the tax; but as auditors, the firm comes only to check the accuracy of the past accounts. The auditors are concerned in no way with the efficiency with which the company is run. Nor are they concerned (apart from the fact that accounts are normally prepared on a 'going concern' basis) with what is likely to happen to the business in the future.

The auditor's role

The auditor's role is emphasised because it is a popular misconception in many small companies that: Our auditors would never let anything happen to us. They would not wish it to and, no doubt, they would warn the directors of impending trouble if they happened to see it, but they are under no obligation either to look for such trouble or to report it.

Furthermore, the operation of quantifying a company's cash needs and generally indoctrinating its staff on liquidity-management techniques is as specialised a subject as any met in the financial discipline. Indeed, outside of the larger sized firms of professional accountants, few possess staff with the necessary practical commercial and industrial expertise to produce a sound professional job.

The legal and moral duties of an auditor in relation to a client company which he considers may be heading for, if not imminent disaster, at least a very severe cash crisis, were considered by the author in an article entitled: 'A task for the auditor — or someone more specialised?', which appeared in the December 1975 edition of *Accountancy*. The following is a short extract:

Few accountants who have been employed in the practising half of

their profession for all of their careers have acquir
'broad view' mentality or the experience and res
running a commercial undertaking. These acc
specialists in their own important and essential fields of a
taxation, liquidations etc. Wise are those of their number who consider themselves as 'GPs' in other specialist financial fields, whose role, like that of the family doctor, is to direct the 'patient' to the right door in the Harley Street of their profession.

These remarks are not intended as the semblance of criticism of the professional auditor, or his role, but rather are meant as a warning to directors not to run their businesses in the belief that their auditor is obligated in some way to be a watchdog over the financial aspects of their company.

Conclusions on the need to plan

The government of the day has a formidable task in convincing the population about the country's economic ills. Financial advisers and consultants have an equally formidable task in convincing many directors of the precarious liquidity position of their companies. Many appear just to turn a deaf ear and to claim, as if it provided a wholly plausible excuse, that they are too busy 'out looking for new customers' — ironically, the one act most likely to exacerbate their illiquidity.

How many directors would happily embark on a voyage knowing that the captain of the ship (*a*) had never checked if there was sufficient fuel aboard and (*b*) was known to face aft and steer the ship merely by looking at the line of the wake?

A prudent traveller on any ship would want to be assured that on the bridge was a team of navigators — 'planners' — who focused their attention on what lay ahead and took account of every known condition likely to be encountered.

Liquidity — the fuel of business

It is the same with business. A company, in this respect, is like a ship. It is totally reliant upon the crew on the bridge. That crew, the senior officers, must not only determine the most appropriate course to steer; they must also ensure there is sufficient fuel on board, sufficient not only to sail straight to the chosen destination but enough to cover any unexpected diversions resulting from storms and other uncontrollable happenings. Liquidity (cash) is the 'business fuel' which a company burns and, like a real ship, it must be expected to burn more when, as now, the conditions are rough.

To survive in business today, the essential requirements include detailed trading plans (against which to order supplies and to monitor progress) and detailed cash forecasts (to ensure sufficient liquidity as and when it will be required in order to meet the obligations of the trading plan).

That survival requires positive action on the part of management should, if there was any doubt, now be clear to the reader. In financial terms, this positive action must stem from knowledge of precisely what is the company's current financial position, and in which direction it is proposing to move in both the short term and the long term.

'Planning' is the key word, so that every facet can be taken into account in designing a complete and viable operation to weather the exterior forces, such as inflation, which are acting against the chances of a successful outcome.

Setting the course

Companies by themselves cannot, of course, cure inflation, but individually they can set a course which will raise materially the chances of survival and offer the opportunity to participate in prosperity when the business climate recovers.

In Parts 3, 4 and 5 of this book, respectively, the funding, the planning and the managing of a company's liquidity needs will be considered in detail.

However, before the reader can fully appreciate the text of this book and the advice given and begin to practise in his own company the methods described, he should have mastered a sound working knowledge of the main terms used in the practical application of liquidity management. Therefore, for those readers who may not be accurately informed on both the definition and relevance of the basic technical jargon, the next section of this book, Part 2, contains not a glossary of all financial terms, but a detailed explanation of the terms which have particular relevance to liquidity management and explains their importance to all businesses whose underlying objective is long-term prosperity.

Part 2

Terminology of liquidity management

3

Definitions and usages

The opening section of this chapter, which briefly describes the principal headings on a balance sheet and the most useful method of layout for planning purposes (containing all the figures in one column) will probably be passed over by professional accountants. All readers, however, may find it beneficial to re-study the descriptions of other terms. Even amongst financial experts, there are some differences of opinion about precisely what is meant, for example, by the 'gearing' of a company.

Balance sheet

It is said one can tell a real professional business manager from the rest by the fact that, given a complete set of accounts, the professional first examines the balance sheet. The majority of people will turn to the trading and profit and loss accounts 'To see what we have sold and how much profit we have made'.

The professional businessman knows that, particularly in times of high inflation, liquidity is as important as profit — hence his trained eye turns first to the balance sheet and the trends of the 'essential ratios' (see below).

The profit and loss account reveals the history of what happened in a period, during which the company traded in buying materials, goods or services at one price and selling them at another price. The balance sheet records not what happened *during* a period, but what the position was *at the end* of that period. But more importantly, the balance sheet shows precisely what the position is at the start of the succeeding period.

The balance sheet's importance, therefore, lies in the insight it gives of the company's ability to face the future. This book will stress again and again the importance of planning future balance sheets with as much care as any other budgeted objectives — here lies the secret of successful liquidity planning. Additionally, these projected balance sheets will provide an advanced measurement of managerial efficiency — before the event has happened, and before any consequential liquidity weaknesses have begun to arise.

Vertical form

Every company has its own peculiarities and there can be no absolute uniformity in the way that company balance sheets are layed out. However, there are many balance sheets which, although not being actually 'wrong', are certainly not helpful to the managements who are supposed to be basing their decisions on such information. Most companies now adopt, whether for financial or management-accounting purposes, a 'vertical form' of balance sheet; alas, the groupings on these are often incorrect, with terms such as 'working capital' being wrongly applied.

The standard balance-sheet layout in Figure 3:1 is given for companies that wish to adopt the basic framework generally found to be of greatest use. Superfluous headings should, of course, be omitted if they are not relevant to a particular company, whilst additional headings which are of particular importance to a business should be added, but added in the appropriate section (eg loan capital should be appropriately classified by term).

Figure 3:1 Standard balance-sheet layout

	£'000	
1	000	Ordinary share capital
2	000	Reserves
3	000	(Adjustment up-dating fixed-asset valuations)
4	000	EQUITY INTEREST
5	000	Preference share capital
6	000	NET WORTH
7	000	Minority interests
8	000	Loan capital (medium and long term)
9	000	Deferred liabilities
10	000	CAPITAL EMPLOYED (Long-term capital)

11	000	Freehold and leasehold property (WDV/cost/value)
12	000	Plant, machinery, vehicles etc (WDV)
13	000	TANGIBLE FIXED ASSETS
14	(000)	(Hire-purchase)
15	000	Goodwill, patents and trade investments
16	000	TOTAL FIXED ASSETS (Long-term assets)
17	000	Net current assets (see below)
18	000	TOTAL NET ASSETS

WORKING CAPITAL (Net current assets)

19	000	Stocks
20	000	Debtors (less doubtful-debt reserve)
21	000	Investments — non-trade
22	000	Cash in hand and at bank
23	000	CURRENT ASSETS
24	000	Trade and expense creditors
25	000	Current taxation
26	000	Dividends payable
27	000	Bank overdraft and short-term loans
28	000	CURRENT LIABILITIES

To avoid any doubt in readers' minds, it is pointed out that this standard balance-sheet layout would not, by itself, comply with the Companies Acts 1948 and 1967 concerning the audited and published annual accounts of limited companies. Such formal financial accounts have to be supported by notes breaking down many of the figures. The standard layout advocated in this book is for internal management purposes only. It will be seen in Part 4 that (*a*) this form is, basically, an all-embracing summary of many working schedules making up the figures, and (*b*) there is a large advantage when month-by-month, or year-by-year, projections are prepared in having all the salient figures contained in just one column.

A number of headings on this balance-sheet layout call for further comment in relation to liquidity management:

(2) *Reserves* — This heading includes both capital reserves (eg share premium account — arising from the issue of shares at a price greater than their face value) and revenue reserves, which term includes not only appropriations to named reserves (eg general reserve) but the 'balance on profit and loss account carried forward' type of heading which was common in accounts until a decade ago. For liquidity-management purposes, these items can all be grouped under one heading which, with the equity share capital forms the backbone to the financial structure of the company.

(3) *Adjustments* — The majority of companies still prepare their accounts on a historical-cost basis. ('Current-cost accounting' is a subject on its own, and not within the compass of this book.) However, in calculating rates of return on the capital employed etc and also what available security the company has to offer, it is more meaningful to take any significant changes in asset valuations into account. Such increases or decreases in value belong to the 'equity shareholders' and should be so placed on the balance sheet that the total of all of the equity shareholders' interests can be aggregated (see heading (4)).

(4) *Equity interest* — This is the total book value (plus any adjustments arising as a result of (3), above) of the shares of those shareholders who do not have any prior rights to either profits or to assets on a winding-up — usually called the 'ordinary shareholders'.

(7) *Minority interests* — This is a term met only in consolidated accounts, and on the balance sheet represents the proportion of the net assets belonging to those parties (the 'outside' shareholders) who own shares in subsidiary companies which are not 'wholly owned' within the group.

(8) *Loan capital* (debentures and other loans) — The term 'debenture' includes debenture stock, mortgage debentures and any other securities of a company, whether they constitute a charge on the assets of the company or not. Debentures are of three kinds:

(*a*) Fixed — the security is on specific assets, the most common being mortgages on properties (both freehold and leasehold). The assets cannot be disposed of by the company unless the secured loan is first repaid.

(*b*) Floating — the security is on a general class of assets which, in the ordinary course of business, is continually changing.

Until steps are taken to enforce the charge the company has the right to continue to deal with the assets.

(*c*) Naked — no security is provided and these debentures are merely acknowledgements of debts due by the company which create no rights beyond those of ordinary unsecured creditors.

(9) *Deferred liabilities* (deferred tax, grants and tax equalisation) — This heading, which may be found with one of many generic titles, includes items which contain an element of long-term liability, but which are not specific borrowings. Taxation payable more than 12 months ahead is often the main constituent. 'Tax equalisation' is an optional adjustment carried out by most companies with a view to equating the charge for depreciation and the tax allowances on their assets. For example, depreciation on plant and machinery is often written off over 10 years in equal instalments; under present legislation, however, the cost may be wholly written off for tax purposes in the first year. Companies adopting a tax-equalisation policy, equate the two on the balance sheet by treating the value of the tax relief obtained in advance of the company's depreciation policy as a potential future liability (increasing the tax charge in the profit and loss account), which is then reduced annually over the expected life of the asset (over the subsequent 9 years in the above example). Neither the creation of a tax-equalisation account nor the movements into and from it each year affect the funds at the company's disposal.

(10) *Capital employed* — This title is often wrongly applied to what is 'net worth' (see line 6). It should be noted that the company's deferred liabilities (including any taxation payable more than 12 months ahead) are included in the total capital employed in the business.

(11) and (12) *Fixed assets* — The Companies Acts require either the cost or valuation figures for classes of assets and their cumulative depreciation to be shown individually; these are best set out in a supporting schedule, with just the net figure(s) appearing on the face of the balance sheet.

(14) *Hire purchase* — Assets on hire-purchase are, legally, only on hire until the end of the contract period — usually three or five years. By custom, the assets of such arrangements are brought into the balance sheet as if they were legally owned by the company, with the instalments still to be paid shown as a deduction (under a separate heading) from the fixed-asset

heading. It is wrong during this period to include all the outstanding instalments as current liabilities (though the agreement may specify a penalty in the event of cancellation).

(17) *Net current assets* — It will be noted that the net working capital (see below) is brought into the balance sheet as a net figure.

(28) *Current liabilities* — For any item to appear under 'current liabilities', it should be payable (or repayable in the case of borrowings) within 12 months of the balance-sheet date. It is all too common a mistake for the current year's instalment on long-term liabilities (e.g. a mortgage loan) to be omitted; such current liabilities must, for financial-management purposes in particular, be transferred from the capital-employed section of the balance sheet. The total of current liabilities is the total amount of the company's short-term liabilities — its 'short-term debt'. Current liabilities are almost always a company's cheapest form of borrowings, but they do represent the highest insolvency risks (creditors, apart from bank borrowings, generally carry no servicing cost except for the possible loss of cash discounts if they are not promptly paid). Current liabilities have due dates for payment for which cash must be available.

Cash flow

The 'positive (or negative) net cash flow' of a business (generally shortened to just 'cash flow') consists of the sum of retained earnings — ie profits less tax and dividends — plus depreciation. Grants and deferred tax may also affect the calculation depending upon how the company treats these items in its accounts (see figure 9:1).

Depreciation is added back because every other item on the profit and loss account concerns the movement of cash at one time or another, into or out of the business. Depreciation (and the amortisation of leases) consists of a book entry by which account is taken of the decrease in value of a fixed asset through use and the lapse of time. The cash aspect of such purchases took place, of course, when the fixed asset was originally bought, and is not reflected in the profit and loss account. In liquidity management one is generally more concerned with cash flow than with profit as such.

In today's highly inflationary climate, cash flow has mainly to be looked to, not ambitiously towards meeting the costs of expanding the business, but to meeting the costs of merely maintaining the existing level of turnover in real terms. It is indeed a fortunate company which has earned a worthwhile surplus after meeting the unavoidable additional investment in working capital arising directly from inflation plus the replacement cost of its essential fixed assets.

Fund statements (sources and uses) are dealt with in Chapter 9; cash flow should not be confused with funding, of which the receipt and expenditure of cash is only a part.

The phrase 'cash flow' is often used in connection with a company's actual day-to-day cash receipts and payments, the planning of which is an essential part of any efficient liquidity-management system. Cash-flow projections are dealt with in Chapter 10.

The phrase is further used in the evaluation of projects and other instances where it is necessary to assess the worth of cash receipts and cost of cash payments at times in the future. 'Discounted cash flows', as this science is generally known, are dealt with in Chapter 8.

Working capital

The expression 'net working capital' is generally shortened to just 'working capital', which more correctly applies only to the total of current assets. Some people distinguish the two by calling them 'net' and 'gross' working capital.

In the context of liquidity management one is working primarily on the individual figures making up the current-assets and liabilities headings, but where the collective term 'working capital' is used in this book, it should, unless otherwise stated, be taken to mean the net working capital — the net current assets of the company (primarily the net difference between stock, debtors and creditors, and either cash or bank overdraft), the items which revolve as the day-to-day business is transacted. Other items, such as current taxation, dividends payable and short-term deposits, government securities etc ('near-cash' items), also, of course, feature in financial considerations of the current position and are reflected in a company's 'working capital'.

It will be seen the working capital (the net figure) represents that proportion of the company's total capital which is employed in its short-term trading operations.

It is important to note that although current assets get converted into cash in the process of trading, at any point in time they often represent a very significant portion of the total capital invested in a company — more so in days of high inflation, when, being of a current nature, stocks and debtors are at almost fully up-dated prices. (In contrast, fixed assets generally appear at historical cost — at prices which often existed before the full effects of the present levels of inflation became evident.)

The liquidity position and the solvency of a company at any point in time are closely related to its current working-capital position. The maintenance of adequate working capital is, therefore, essential to the well-being of every business — and the relationship between the main components is of equal importance. For example, creditors will not take kindly to a suggestion that they be paid in kind because the company has too much stock and no spare cash.

The control of working capital, as will be seen in Chapter 13, is best dealt with through the monitoring of the six 'essential ratios' (listed below).

Current ratio (or working-capital ratio)

This is simply the ratio of total current assets to total current liabilities, and is a crude measure of the safety margin afforded to the company's short-term creditors.

Custom varies with the type of trade and size of business, but a ratio of not less than 1.5:1 is desirable. For example, £150,000 of current assets to not more than £100,000 of current liabilities.

Obviously, the portion of the current assets which is not covered by current liabilities (£50,000 in the example above) must be financed out of long-term capital — out of the 'capital-employed' figure, which is not, therefore, entirely available to finance fixed assets.

Creditors, particularly bankers, become apprehensive when they see the current ratio dropping below 1.5:1, because this signals to them that the extra security afforded by the long-term capital backing of the business has been used elsewhere, leaving their debt covered by a possibly inadequate margin of trading assets. These trading assets are:

1 Stock which, unless it is mainly comprised of commodities dealt in on a recognised exchange, does not generally possess a quickly realisable value near to the figure appearing in the balance sheet
2 Debtors which, even if 'doubtful debts' are fully provided for, will almost certainly take many months to collect.

Although, in terms of their quickly realisable values, current assets may fall short of the figures appearing in the balance sheet, generally speaking they realise a higher percentage of their face value than do fixed assets on a forced sale of an undertaking.

Quick ratio

This ratio is also known as either the liquid ratio or the quick asset ratio. It is derived from the same items as comprise the current ratio, but omits stock. Again, custom varies with the type of trade and size of business, but a ratio of not less than 1:1 is desirable. Therefore, of the £150,000 of current assets, in the example discussed in the section on the current ratio above, not more than £50,000 should be held in stock.

Considering the current ratio and the quick ratio together, it will be seen arithmetically that, ideally, the value of stock should be entirely financed out of long-term capital. Thus, short-term creditors (trade and expense creditors, current taxation, dividends payable, bank overdraft, etc) should be balanced by debtors (less provision for doubtful debts), cash at bank and any 'near-cash' items (short-term investments) such as deposits or government stock.

This is a relationship which would please a banker, but is not often found in practice — especially not in manufacturing companies, where the finance tied up in raw materials, work-in-progress and finished goods can be formidable.

A quick ratio of less than 1:1 will indicate an 'illiquid' position under which creditors must expect the company to take extended credit and, in the case of bank borrowings, not necessarily to be able to honour agreed reductions. Applying this test to a balance sheet, particularly to that of a customer seeking more credit, is often referred to as 'applying the acid test'. (One of the problems of published accounts is that they show the financial position at only one point of time in the year — often many months out of date — and that time may not be typical for the whole year; most businesses are seasonal to some degree, and the relationship between liquid and illiquid assets can change significantly without the knowledge of third parties.)

Stock ratio

This ratio is designed primarily to indicate whether a company is carrying too much stock or, expressed differently, whether its stock is being turned over as often either as it is planned to be or as other companies in the same trade (statistics from trade associations can be very useful in this latter respect).

As was indicated when discussing working capital, above, particularly in times of high inflation, a very large proportion of a company's capital can become tied up virtually permanently, and unremuneratively, if efforts are not made to minimise the stock which is carried. Methods for lessening the level of stocks are considered in Chapter 6.

It is common to find two methods of expressing the turnover of stock. For example, a company with an annual cost-of-sales figure of, say, £400,000 has stocks of £100,000. It may then be said either: (*a*) that the company is carrying 3 months of stock (i.e. on average, it turns its stock over once every 3 months):

$$\frac{\pounds 100{,}000}{\pounds 400{,}000} \times 12 \text{ months} = 3 \text{ months}$$

or (*b*) that the company has a 'stock turnround' of 4 (ie on average, it turns its stock over 4 times a year):

$$\frac{\pounds 400{,}000}{\pounds 100{,}000} = 4$$

Three important points should be noted:

1 The turnover figure utilised is 'cost of sales' not, as many companies quite incorrectly use, their sales turnover which is, of course, at selling price. (Gross profit margins vary both company to company and generally between products sold by the same company)
2 The stock-valuation figure utilised should be the average over the period covered by the cost-of-sales figure. In most cases, an average of the opening and closing stock levels will be found to be of sufficient accuracy, but where there is a seasonal factor involved a more sophisticated form of weighted average is needed
3 Non-trading forms of stock, such as stationery, fuel and packing materials, should be deducted if they are included in the global stock figure

The level of stock carried should bear a close relationship with sales and orders in hand, and should not materially exceed what is necessary to meet customers' reasonable demands, taking into account all abnormal demands arising from special advertising campaigns, seasonal influences and the like.

The ratio of stock to cost of sales can vary widely depending upon the type of business, the length of the manufacturing processes involved etc. But whatever the normal ratio is in a particular company, it is one which should be monitored constantly (both within the company and with the published results of other similar companies), with every effort being made to improve it.

Idle stock and obsolete stock costs money, and therefore profits, and can render otherwise useless very large proportions of a company's liquid resources in a badly managed organisation.

Debtors ratio

This ratio (usually expressed in 'numbers of days' sales') is designed primarily to indicate whether a company is granting its customers too much credit — generally as a result of inefficient credit control.

This ratio is derived basically from the relationship between turnover (omitting cash sales) and the as yet unpaid portion of those sales (debtors). It is surprising, however, to find that with all their other sophistication, probably 75 per cent of companies incorrectly calculate this ratio. The majority do this from average figures which renders the resulting ratios at best inaccurate and at worst grossly misleading.

Only if a company has a constant level of turnover throughout the year, and this is very rarely found, should current total debtors be related either to annual sales or to an average thereof with a view to determining the 'average age' of the debts.

A simple example will demonstrate this fallacy. A company has the following sales:

Month		Month	
1	£10,000	7	£30,000
2	£10,000	8	£30,000
3	£15,000	9	£40,000
4	£15,000	10	£40,000
5	£20,000	11	£10,000
6	£20,000	12	£10,000

Total sales for year: £250,000

If its debtors at the end of months 4 and 10 were both £40,000, protagonists of relating debtors to the year's turnover would say in both cases that 58.4 days' sales were outstanding:

$$\frac{\pounds\ 40{,}000}{\pounds 250{,}000} \text{ x } 365 \text{ days} = 58.4 \text{ days}$$

But a quick examination of the facts shows this not to be either a correct statement or a relevant one as a controlling discipline. At the end of month 4, debtors of £40,000 represented three whole months of sales at the most recent rate of selling, while at the end of month 10, debtors of £40,000 represented only one month at the then current selling rate.

For this ratio to be meaningful as one of the six essential ratios of liquidity management, it should reflect time in terms of the most recent sales effected. The statistic should normally be calculated by deducting those months' sales, commencing with the most recent, which in total can be deducted from the total debtors figure. The balance left over is then expressed (in days to one decimal place) as a fraction of the next previous month's sales.

Small 'debit balances' often arise on the bought ledger or month-end 'accruals schedule' (eg the prepayment of insurance premiums) which in the financial accounts are added to debtors. This is inconvenient for management-accounting purposes and it is suggested that any such expense prepayments be deducted from expense creditors — see the next section.

Value added tax

There is one other trap awaiting the unwary. If a company has to add VAT to its sales, then its debtors will be inflated relative to the sales figures appearing in the management accounts and statistics. In these circumstances, therefore, in order to obtain the correct debtors ratio, the monthly sales figures taken into the calculation should be increased by the appropriate VAT rate (or rates). It should be noted that VAT is not chargeable on any overseas sales included in the total; further, either VAT may not be applicable on all the company's UK sales or it may not be chargeable on all those sales at the same rate.

It should be noted that, in arithmetical terms, debtors are equal to the sum of (*a*) the stock which they previously represented and (*b*) the gross profit margin arising on those sales (plus VAT if applicable). This statement may appear as being too simple to warrant making, but in liquidity terms there is a special significance. The mere transfer (by delivery and by invoicing) of £*X* of goods out of stock (at cost price) and into debtors (at selling price) does not of itself call for any change in the requirement for liquidity resources. However, this 'transfer' affects the total of current assets and, therefore, also affects both the current ratio and the quick ratio. The significance of this will be considered in Chapter 13.

Trade creditors ratio

This ratio (usually expressed in 'numbers of days' purchases') is designed primarily to ensure that a company is not paying its creditors either (*a*) unnecessarily early or (*b*) unreasonably late.

Many companies prepare so-called creditors ratios which are of little value; this is because the figures used are in respect of only those items which 'go through' the bought ledger. Very often a lot of expense items, the VAT and perhaps even the PAYE feature in the liability figure which is then erroneously related to just the manufacturing and trading account purchases.

In practice, it is convenient for the bought ledger to be operated in two parts, one which relates wholly to trade purchases (raw materials or goods for resale) and one which covers all the expense and sundry items. There is generally no point in producing monthly ratios on the latter classification since there is little consistency throughout the year on the incidence of many large items such as rent, rates and insurances. Only when forecasting several year-end figures for the future (ie comparing several ratios, each taken at the same period of time — see Figure 9:2) can it be meaningful to group the trade creditors with the expense creditors.

The trade creditors ratio should be calculated similarly to the debtors ratio with the creditors being related, not to the average rate of purchases, but to the most recent months' figures. Also as in the case of the debtors ratio, the monthly purchases should be increased by an appropriate amount for VAT, which of course features in most creditor figures.

Profit ratio

The sixth and last of the essential ratios is that concerning the gross profitability earned by a company — the difference between its sales and the direct cost to the company of those sales — its profit margin.

In a wholesale or retail company, where finished goods are bought at one price then sold at another, the identification of the gross margin is simple.

For a manufacturing company, perhaps encompassing many different processes at all of which various oncosts (to cover production overheads) may be added, the identification is not always straightforward. In management terms in these situations it is often more desirable to monitor gross profitability at the individual division, process or plant stages.

Pricing and the need to achieve minimum profit levels will be considered later, but the reader must be able to distinguish clearly between a 'profit percentage' and a 'markup', the latter generally being expressed as a percentage of the cost of sale while the former is, of course, given in terms of the selling price. Some simple examples will make this clear:

	(A)	(B)	(C)
Sale price	£100	£100	£100
Cost of sale	50	75	80
Gross profit	£ 50	£ 25	£ 20

In example:

(A) The profit percentage is 50 per cent and the markup is 100 per cent
(B) The profit percentage is 25 per cent and the markup is 33⅓ per cent
(C) The profit percentage is 20 per cent and the markup is 25 per cent

The emphasis here on identifying the gross profit is not to imply that it is the only trading margin of importance. The difference between the gross and net margins, taking a company as a whole, is represented by its 'overheads', a change in the level of which will have a direct, indeed absolute, effect on the resulting profit (£100 extra of overhead costs will result in £100 less of pre-tax profits).

In the short-term, overheads are best controlled as actual amounts against predetermined standards (budgets) according to their classification as (*a*) variable, (*b*) semivariable, or (*c*) fixed. However, in drawing up corporate plans (see Chapter 7) or when reviewing a company's past achievements over a number of years, it can be pertinent to highlight the underlying trends by relating either total overheads (excluding, of course, finance charges) or net trading profits to sales in the form of simple ratios.

Overtrading

'Legal insolvency' is when a company's third-party liabilities exceed the value of all of its assets. Where, to the knowledge of the directors, there is no reasonable prospect of the company's debts being paid, it is generally held that the company is being carried on with intent to defraud its creditors. Therefore, unless the directors are prepared to run the risk of being called upon personally to meet the excess debts of their company, they should cease to trade well before a position of 'legal insolvency' is reached.

'Overtrading' is an imprecisely defined state of affairs — sometimes called 'technical insolvency' — when a company has sufficient assets to meet all its financial obligations, but neither sufficient ready cash nor sufficient time in which to convert its other assets into cash in order to meet its debts as they fall due. Creditors become apprehensive and often worsen the situation by curtailing credit.

It is possible, therefore, for a company to make substantial profits while it is technically insolvent — ie its profits are not available in liquid form.

Ironically, it is prosperity itself that so often brings down a company. Managements become bemused by the opportunity presented by an unexpected demand for their products and, in the absence of a strong hand on the financial helm, mass production is begun with little thought about how the time-lag between buying stocks of raw materials, manufacturing work-in-progress and finally collecting the cash from debtors is to be financed.

A company has to be solvent to be able to remain in existence. Profitability, it has been seen, does not of itself ensure a sufficient degree of solvency. On the other hand, it is not necessary to be so liquid that all debts can be paid off immediately. It is only necessary to be able to become sufficiently liquid should the need arise.

Conversely, an unprofitable company is not necessarily insolvent — it may be able to continue paying its debts even if a part of its share capital is lost.

'Liquid resources' are idle resources, and much of the skill of liquidity management is centred on maintaining the optimum level of this valuable, but all too ephemeral, commodity.

Classes of shares

Except in the smaller companies, it is usual to find more than one 'class' of shareholders enjoying different rights to one another. But it must be emphasised that the names ascribed to such classes are only general indications of their characteristics, and only by examining the company's memorandum and articles of association will all the rights and obligations of the holders be found.

There are virtually an unlimited number of variations to the types of shares a company can have. The following are the most common:

1 *Preference shares* — these usually carry preferential rights as regards

both dividends (they may be entitled to a fixed rate of dividend before any payment is made to other classes of shareholders) and on a return of capital on a winding-up (but unless this right is specifically conferred on the holders by the memorandum and articles of association of the company, the preference shares are repaid *pari passu* with the ordinary shares — the ordinary shares usually enjoying the whole of any final surplus).

2 *Redeemable preference shares* — these carry the obligation on the company to repay them either all on a fixed date or a given number each year. Such obligations must be allowed for in liquidity management and it must not be overlooked that such redemptions can, by law, only be paid out of either (*a*) profits which the company would otherwise have available for the payment of dividends or (*b*) the proceeds of a new issue of shares.

3 *Participating preference shares* — these carry the right to an extra dividend (above the preferential fixed percentage) once the ordinary shareholders have, in any year, been paid a given percentage.

4 *Ordinary shares* — these take the surplus profits after all prior interests have been met; a part of such 'surplus profit' will generally be distributed by way of dividend with the balance being retained to augment the capital employed within the company.

Gearing

What is meant when the term 'gearing' is used is not, unfortunately, the same for every person concerned with finance. Basically, the word should be used (as in (1) below) to relate, on the one hand, capital sources which carry a fixed interest entitlement to those which, on the other hand, carry the residual claim on profits and assets.

The term may be found comparing medium- and long-term debt with any of the following:

1 Funds belonging to the equity shareholders
2 Total net worth
3 Total capital employed

The 'gearing' given by the three definitions, based on the figures in Figure 3:2, would be:

1 £600,000 : £1,500,000 = 40%
2 £600,000 : £2,000,000 = 30%
3 £600,000 : £3,000,000 = 20%

Figure 3:2 The gearing in capital employed

	£'000
Ordinary share capital	800
Reserves	700
EQUITY INTEREST	1,500
Preference share capital	500
NET WORTH	2,000
Debenture stock	600
Deferred taxation etc	400
CAPITAL EMPLOYED	3,000

Of the three, the most usually adopted measurement is the first, and this will be the form of the relationship of debt to other expressions of capital meant by gearing when the term is used in this book.

It is a commonly heard claim of successful business entrepreneurs that they reached their success by using other people's money (rather than their own, or because they had no personal capital). But if a group of bankrupt entrepreneurs were asked to what they attributed their failure, the chances are that many would say because they borrowed and became overcommitted.

It is the same with companies. To borrow is to increase the risks; to fail to borrow is to defer, possibly indefinitely, the chances of real success. Provided borrowing commitments are limited to a company's availability of security and interest cover, gearing should be in the long-term interests of the shareholders provided profits are at least maintained. Figure 3:3 shows the effect gearing can have on the earnings of ordinary shareholders in a simply capitalised company when profits are either doubled or halved.

Figure 3:3 Effect of gearing on earnings

	Type of capital employed	
	All ordinary	100% geared
	£'000	£'000
Ordinary share capital	1,000	500
12% Loan stock		500
	1,000	1,000

	Type of capital employed	
	All ordinary £'000	100% geared £'000
(A) Net profit before tax and interest	300	300
Loan interest	—	60
	300	240
Taxation at 50%	150	120
Available for ordinary shareholders	150	120
Earnings on ordinary shares	15%	24%
(B) *Doubled profits*		
Net profit before tax and interest	600	600
Loan interest	—	60
	600	540
Taxation at 50%	300	270
Available for ordinary shareholders	300	270
Earnings on ordinary shares	30%	54%
(C) *Halved profits*		
Net profit before tax and interest	150	150
Loan interest	—	60
	150	90
Taxation at 50%	75	45
Available for ordinary shareholders	75	45
Earnings on ordinary shares	7.5%	9%

However, gearing does not, in terms of debt, necessarily always mean only long-term borrowings. A company can be said to be 'highly geared' with no borrowings in its 'capital-employed' total, but with, for example, a very large overdraft or other short-term debt. The borrowings ratio reflects this type of gearing and relates the total of all borrowings to net worth.

Cost of supporting debt

When considering the proportion of a company's capital which should be funded by (*a*) permanent capital and (*b*) debt, the relevance of the following further points at least should be assessed:

1 Debt entails legal obligations to pay interest on due dates (generally half-yearly) and to make capital repayments of the sum borrowed (the 'principal') either at specified dates over the period of the loan or at the end of the period. These legal obligations represent a potential threat to a company's solvency in the event of a severe, albeit temporary, decline in profits
2 Unsecured loan stock is generally issued on the basis of a company's earnings, with lenders looking for an interest cover of not less than 4 or 5 times (ie profits before tax and before such interest need to be equal to 4 or 5 times that interest charge)
3 Debentures (secured loan stock) are primarily issued on the basis of a company's assets though, of course, its earnings record is also assessed carefully by a would-be lender
4 Interest is 'tax deductible' (ie the charge is allowed as a deduction against profits before the resulting 'assessable profit' is taken as the basis for calculating the company's liability to corporation tax). Dividends are not 'tax deductible' but the amount of cash the company actually pays to shareholders out of its after-tax profit is, under the imputation system of tax, treated as a net-of-tax receipt in the shareholders' hands (see Figure 3:4).

Therefore, a company's ability to support debt is primarily a function of its earnings not its assets alone. The assets may be mortgaged in order to raise the loan, but the loan is paid for solely out of earnings (ie servicing costs; also redemption unless the loan is to be replaced by a substitute form of capital). Only as a result of either bad financial management or catastrophy striking the company will secured debts be repaid by means of the forced sale of the assets on which they are charged.

In the example in Figure 3:4, it will be seen that, in terms of retained earnings the result for the company is the same in both columns, but in

Figure 3:4 Distribution of geared and ungeared profits

	Capital not geared £'000	Capital geared £'000
Trading profit	1,000	1,000
Interest charge	—	250
Net profit before tax	1,000	750
Taxation at 50%	500	375
Net profit after tax	500	375
Dividend	250	125
Retained earnings	250	250
Income received by:		
Shareholders:		
Net cash dividend	250	125
Grossing up at 35%	135	67
	385	192
Debenture holders (gross)	—	250
Total gross income	385	442

terms of total gross income, the financial backers (the shareholders and debenture holders) obtained more from the geared company than from the ungeared one. The difference has been made up by the Revenue and points to a means whereby it can be beneficial for those who are prepared to put funds into a company to consider reducing the share element in favour of a part-debt structure. (There is legislation which prevents this apparent loophole from being exploited in the case of 'close companies'.)

Gearing under inflationary conditions
Increased advantages to borrowers come into play under inflationary

conditions, with corresponding disadvantages to lenders. The force at work here is, of course, the purchasing power of the cash which is borrowed.

Take a simple case of a five-year loan which is to be repaid in equal instalments at the end of each of the five years. Assuming inflation at a constant 25 per cent a year, in 'real terms' there is, as compared with the original loan, an arithmetical capital gain of some 46 per cent (Figure 3:5).

Figure 3:5 'Real terms' cost of repaying a loan

		Monetary terms	'Real terms' basis
Year 0	Borrow	£100,000	£100,000
Year 1 (end)	Repay	20,000	16,000
		80,000	84,000
Year 2 (end)	Repay	20,000	12,800
		60,000	71,200
Year 3 (end)	Repay	20,000	10,200
		40,000	61,000
Year 4 (end)	Repay	20,000	8,200
		20,000	52,800
Year 5 (end)	Repay	20,000	6,600
			£ 46,200

On the face of it, such a borrowing almost takes on the appearance of a fraud, borrowing one sum of money and later paying back slightly more than half in full satisfaction. It is little wonder that there is a general unwillingness to lend cash. However, banks seem quite prepared to continue lending their depositors' cash out on such terms.

In these conditions, interest considerations can almost be overlooked; they are small in relation to the loss of value of the principal and, in any case, generally about half the interest reward is lost to taxation.

In Chapter 6, the advantages of utilising existing assets to raise loans, which can then be repaid with cash of a lower purchasing power, is examined.

Unless required for a specific and fairly immediate purpose, the costing of which has taken full account of both the 'opportunity cost' and the fall in purchasing power, surplus cash should never be kept in liquid form since its worth in real terms diminishes daily.

The principles to follow under inflationary conditions are epitomised in the maxim: Own what is going up; owe what is going down (ie most tangible assets are appreciating in value; cash loans are having their purchasing power eroded).

Maintaining flexibility

Later in this book, the desirability of maintaining flexibility will be seen to discourage unnecessary long-term borrowings. A company's security is always limited and it is prudent to ration its borrowings to produce the best returns. Current opportunities may be inferior to those which will shortly present themselves. Additionally, if a company has borrowed up to the hilt, it has little chance of weathering any temporary recessions.

Also, in so far as investing in inessential assets is concerned, fashions may change. The best example being, of course, property. How many companies overextended their resources in the early 1970s in order to buy (rather than be left out) during the 'property boom'? Many companies which bought late are, at best, now faced with substantial paper losses and, at worst, have been forced to realise, at a considerable loss, what was regarded, traditionally, as about the safest of investments.

Borrowing powers

It is not uncommon to find many companies with no borrowing limits imposed upon their management by their articles of association.

Table A of the Companies Act 1948, which is the basis of the articles for the great majority of companies, contains under regulation 79 the following:

> The directors may exercise all the powers of the company to borrow money, and to mortgage or charge its undertaking, property and uncalled capital, or any part thereof, and to issue debentures, debenture stock, and other securities whether outright or as security for any debt, liability or obligation of the company or of any third party:
>
> Provided that the amount for the time being remaining

> undischarged of moneys borrowed or secured by the directors as aforesaid (apart from temporary loans obtained from the company's bankers in the ordinary course of business) shall not at any time, without the previous sanction of the company in general meeting, exceed the nominal amount of the share capital of the company for the time being issued . . .

Probably the majority of companies adopting Table A (with or without other variations of their own) will either exclude regulation 79 altogether (thereby electing to operate without any limit) or substitute a more liberal restriction for it. It is not uncommon to find substituted a limit such as 'A sum equal to':

1 The paid-up share capital plus reserves according to the latest published accounts, or
2 The paid-up share capital plus reserves multiplied by a factor, say 1½ or 2

It is the obligation of every director to ensure his company is operating within its various powers — and one of the most important of these is its 'borrowing powers'. Bank managers always require to see a copy of a company's articles of association before they will open an account. Would-be lenders should always call for the articles, and should also seek the total of current borrowings to be certified by the auditors.

If, for liquidity-management purposes a higher level of borrowings than is permitted by the articles is required, the shareholders should be approached and the formality of changing the articles will have to be carried through by means of a special resolution.

It should not be overlooked that a borrowings limit is placed on companies for a purpose. No shareholder should accept lightly that the directors propose either to remove the limit altogether or to extend it. The limit is designed to ensure that the management does not 'over-gear' the company to the potential detriment of the shareholders (and, of course, the creditors) who would bear the loss if the additional risk of such increased borrowings were found to have been ill-judged. The directors, even of small private companies, should be required to make out a proper case for seeking such increased powers.

In practical terms, with the value of preference shares generally standing well below par, the greatest opposition to changing articles of association today must be expected to come from the preference shareholders. Their rights, if any, to block such resolutions can be ascertained from the company's articles. If they have such a power they may well seek an uplift of the rate of their fixed dividend as a quid pro quo for voting in favour of a change — a change which would be most likely to favour the ordinary shareholders.

Borrowing powers should be checked periodically since they are fundamental to a company's ability to borrow for the purpose of improving liquidity management. Additionally, the total of all classes of borrowings falling within the definition of the company's own articles of association should be scheduled periodically and formally submitted by the company secretary to the directors, say, quarterly at a board meeting, where the position should be noted in the minutes.

Part 3

Surveying the funding options

Before it is practical to consider either the detailed planning of a company's liquidity (dealt with in Part 4) or the management of a company's finances (dealt with in Part 5), it is, for the reader:

1 Useful to be able to distinguish between the broad types of situation which give rise to a company needing the injection of additional funds, and
2 Essential to know what types of finance, and their respective costs, may be available.

4

Requirements for funds

This chapter considers the types of situation which can give rise to an unavoidable need for additional funds.

Fixed and current assets

The main object of being in business is to make profits. The cost of being in business is the necessary investment in assets, without which the business cannot function. To be in a position to acquire such assets, the company must have funds (often also called finance) with which to meet the cost, but such funds do not necessarily have to be in the form of cash. For example, creditors may agree to provide credit, albeit short-term, which enables the company to take delivery of materials and goods without having first to pay out any of its liquid funds.

Assets are of two types:

1 Current assets, which represent the cost of actually doing business (ie trading)
2 Fixed assets, which represent the cost of being in business

The purpose of each is quite different and so, also, are their respective characteristics and liquidity management considerations:

1 *Current assets* are held for the minimum of time, goods and materials being bought for either resale or manufacture into marketable products. The management of current assets — primarily stock and debtors — generally revolves around liquidity considerations.
2 *Fixed assets* are bought for the long term and call, before commitment to purchase, for both careful strategic planning and financial appraisal in terms of 'use' and 'return'. Their worth to the

company effectively revolves around technical considerations; they have low liquidity and are not bought with a view to resale. They should be wholly financed by long term capital.

Undercapitalised?

The most obvious situation which calls for additional funds is when the company is employing insufficient long-term Capital.

This situation can arise from a number of reasons, for example:

Insufficiency of share capital:

1 When formed, an inaccurate assessment was made of the company's immediate financial needs
2 Expansion of the company's business has not been matched either by sufficient retentions of profits or by the introduction of new capital
3 The founders of the company, possibly a family, refuse to surrender control (they may even refuse to give up any portion of the equity), effectively putting a block on the issue of new shares in the absence of surplus funds of their own
4 The profits have been so low (losses may have been made) that it is impossible to attract new equity investors
5 The märket (Stock Exchange) conditions may be such that no new equity can be raised by rights issues or otherwise
6 Actual losses on either trading or disposing of fixed assets have permanently depleted the share-capital base
7 Redeemable shares reached maturity at a time when a substitute form of share funding was impossible

Insufficiency of loan capital:

1 The company has insufficient assets of the type and value necessary for the purpose of securing new loan capital
2 The company has an inadequate profit record so that there would be insufficient cover for the interest on any new borrowings
3 The cost of new loan capital would be such as to make it unattractive for the company to enter a long-term commitment on current terms

What is the right level of long-term capital for a company to have? It was seen in Chapter 3, that the total of 'capital employed' has not only to finance the fixed assets of the company, but also the working capital (the net difference between the current assets and the current liabilities).

Rules of thumb

The requirements for long-term capital, in order to meet a part of the investment in stocks and debtors, largely depends upon the type of business (a retail shop selling for cash cannot, for example, have the same 'rule of thumb' applied to it as, say, a construction company which has to provide long-term credit).

The 'capital employed' (total figure as defined in Chapter 3) should, as a general rule of guidance, be adjusted to equal the necessary levels of:

fixed assets plus ⅓ of current assets

The reader is referred to Chapter 3 — 'Current Ratio'.

There cannot, however, be any rule of thumb about the most desirable relationship between the working-capital and the fixed-asset requirements. For example, two otherwise identical companies would have very different requirements if one leased its property while the other owned its own freehold.

In times of financial strain, managements often seek to bridge what they hope is only a temporary deficiency, by introducing short-term capital in the form, for example, of an increased overdraft facility. But these measures are seldom effective in such circumstances, and tend to weaken the whole financial structure and, therefore, the standing of the company (see Chapter 3 — 'Quick Ratio').

For a company to try to operate with the object of being successful in the long-term, an adequate level of either permanent or semi-permanent capital is essential.

Examples of two companies, one with an insufficiency of capital employed and one which meets the normal requirements for current and quick ratios is given in Figure 4:1.

Figure 4:1 Companies with (A) inadequate and (B) adequate long-term capital

	Company (A)	Company (B)
	£'000	£'000
NET WORTH	1,000	1,000
Long-term loans	—	600
CAPITAL EMPLOYED	1,000	1,600
Fixed assets	1,200	1,200
Net current assets	—	400
Net current liabilities	200	—
TOTAL NET ASSETS	1,000	1,600

	Company (A) £'000	Company (B) £'000
WORKING CAPITAL		
Stock	400	400
Debtors	600	600
Cash at bank	—	200
Current assets	1,000	1,200
Trade and expense creditors, taxation and dividends	800	800
Overdraft	400	—
Current liabilities	1,200	800
Current ratio	0.83	1.50
Quick ratio	0.50	1.00

To compute the requirement for long-term capital in order to finance a company's working capital, it is necessary to proceed along the lines described at the end of Chapter 9.

Insolvency

It might be thought that the previous subheading ('Undercapitalised?') would have encompassed all considerations concerning the requirements for funds, but there are a number of special situations which call for individual comment.

The first of these is when the company is in either a legally insolvent state or a technically insolvent one. (Readers are referred to Chapter 3 for a full description of each.)

Legal insolvency

Legal insolvency, when third-party liabilities exceed the value of all the company's assets, is generally only soluble if either the equity shareholders are prepared to make good the deficiency or the company is taken over.

Legal insolvency does not necessarily bring about immediate liquidation. The various classes of creditors have a prior claim on the business assets, and it is not uncommon for them to apply for the company to be carried on under a 'receiver and manager' with a view to its ultimate and beneficial sale as a going concern.

Technical insolvency
Technical insolvency (overtrading) stems from too fast an expansion of the company relative to the capacity of its capital to cope with financing a commensurable increase in working capital.

The state of technical insolvency is not difficult to correct with an appropriate injection of funds. However, the provider of such funds will require to be assured that the management is capable of preventing the same situation building up again. A tight rein needs to be put on the directors with the installation of an efficient liquidity-management 'early warning' system as one essential condition of the loan.

Expansion

When a significant expansion of a company's turnover is being contemplated, care must be taken to ensure that the major portion of the extra funds is introduced in at least a semi-permanent form — ie as medium- or long-term debt. This is particularly so when such expansion requires not only a greater investment in working capital, but also in fixed assets.

Short-term needs may be financed by short-term funds, but if this form is used as the principal source, it limits very considerably the scope the directors have for raising long-term debt if either the opportunity to expand even more rapidly offers itself or the existing funds prove to have been underestimated.

Growth can come from both (*a*) an expansion of the existing basic business (eg increasing its sales in the present market, moving into new territories, introducing new selling methods) and (*b*) the addition of a quite different range of goods.

Existing business
With the possible exception of introducing new selling methods (eg introducing mail order in addition to normal credit selling), expansion of the existing basic business will generally give rise to a directly proportional increase in debtors, but not necessarily to any increase in stock. Stock levels may, for example, be able to absorb a volume increase of, say, 10 per cent or more in sales without lowering the standard of service given to customers.

Stock levels will need to be increased if the expansion is planned to come from new territories which necessitate working from additional depots, warehouses etc. All other considerations apart, there is no reason why suppliers (trade creditors) should not finance the usual proportion of the expected increase in the stocks.

New products

The addition of an entirely new range of products, however, will not only give rise to a likely increase in net working capital, but may also involve new capital expenditure.

Provided an expansion of turnover is properly planned, the necessary funds arranged well in advance and its development carefully monitored, an overtrading situation should never arise. (The reader's attention is particularly drawn to Chapter 2 — 'The Financial Requirement in Marketing'.)

Managements are sometimes heard trying to justify their overtrading on grounds of 'Having to make money while we can'. What they really have in mind is 'Making profits while we can'. Ironically, if they really did concentrate on the money aspect, and stopped to realise that money is not synonymous with profit, their companies would be more healthy in liquidity terms.

Capital needed to support growth

Capital, not just profits, is the basic requirement to support growth which should, in turn, yield a higher level of profitability at a later date.

But preparedness is an essential ingredient, and managements should have contingency plans worked out well in advance. Such plans must be realistic and allow for an entirely different result manifesting itself. Having worked for many months, possibly even years, on forecasts, estimates, budgets and targets it is possible to become so bemused with the 'crystal ball' results as to believe they are virtually guaranteed. Nothing could be further from the truth.

Entrepreneurial

'Green-field' situations are really outside the scope of this book, though this is not to imply that entrepreneurs would not be well advised to practise liquidity-management techniques from the outset.

The record of entrepreneurs with the institutions has not been an encouraging one, and many of the merchant banks have now closed their 'venture capital' sections.

But venture capital is available. Additionally, most directors of established firms will find themselves being approached from time to time with propositions to back.

Entrepreneurs, as a breed, are notoriously parsimonious about giving up portions of their shares: 'Just lend us the cash' is the usual request. If an apparently worthwhile proposition is offered to an established organisation, more often than not it will be better to take the new entity into the group as a subsidiary company, possibly satisfying the founder's demands for control with an agreement to issue, and then buy back, further shares depending upon the level of success achieved.

Providing venture capital

A company which decides to back an entrepreneur should bear a few principles in mind:

1 The amount 'invested' should be no more than what can be regarded by that company as expendable. It is claimed that no more than 1 in 10 ventures ever reach the full expectations of their backers, while perhaps 50 per cent lose their investment
2 Such 'investments' will almost certainly call for a disproportionately high amount of management time by way of supervision, counselling etc
3 The need for finance must be assessed carefully before any commitment is entered into. Most entrepreneurs have the weirdest ideas about how much cash is needed to develop and launch a new venture. To provide less funds than really are required is worse for all parties than not becoming involved at all
4 If the company tries to tie the entrepreneur down too precisely the arrangement will be doomed from the start. By their nature, entrepreneurs are very individualistic people and do not easily work creatively under too much red tape
5 While the company should not take advantage and overload the enterprise with unfair parent-company overheads, there is little point to either side in producing a wholly false picture as a result of not charging the new venture with all its justifiable costs (eg if accommodation belonging to the parent company is being occupied, a reasonable charge for rent, heat, light etc. should be made)

Finally, an established company which is itself experiencing liquidity problems, should *never* embark upon venture-capital situations. Its own bankers and other would-be lenders are likely to take a wholly unsympathetic view towards supporting a company in order that it, in turn, can continue its support of one or more somewhat dubious, and as yet unproved, venture-capital projects.

Lenders' criteria

> There are almost as many definitions of the word 'profit' as there are words in the English dictionary.

This bold statement cynically expresses the author's views after listening to, and later examining, the introductory claims of a great many businessmen and would-be businessmen. People whose ideas on the ease with which true 'profits' can be made are matched only by the inevitability of their own assured failure were other parties to be so foolish as to make them the 'temporary loans' they say, and in most cases no doubt honestly think, is all that stands between them and instant wealth.

That commerce and industry do employ many a fool is probably undeniable, but the presence of so many half-baked schemes does make it that much harder for the genuine borrower's proposition, particularly when approaching an entirely new source for funds, to obtain immediate recognition. All the more reason, therefore, that such requests as do justify sympathetic consideration should be presented in a manner which immediately alerts the receiver to give them his full time and attention.

Professional presentation

The case should be presented professionally which, for all but the largest groups, inevitably means employing professionally trained experts to help prepare it and to be present to support it. As much relevant written data as possible should be sent ahead of the initial meeting with a view to convincing the potential lender that the case has been well thought through and is plausible both as regards (*a*) its main objectives and (*b*) the indicated terms for the requested facility (interest cover, security and repayment provisions). Only then should the management, upon whom the lender would have to rely to achieve the planned objectives, be introduced in person. The meeting should preferably be at the company's principal place of work, where an experienced lender will quickly detect an air of purpose and efficiency, if such pervades.

Space does not permit a detailed consideration of what information should and should not be supplied, but before any loan is likely to be agreed to, the lender will need to be satisfied, among other considerations, about whether:

1 The management is of sufficient calibre in every necessary discipline to match the challenge
2 The products and the markets at which they are aimed are compatible, that the existence of a demand for such products has been evidenced and such demand is not subject to wide fluctuations
3 The accounting facilities are accurate, up-to-date and capable of handling efficiently what will be required of them
4 The liquidity requirements have been quantified accurately and on a moderately conservative basis
5 The financial controls are such that progress will be monitored regularly and any adverse trends will be quickly detected.

A good track record generally, and a sound set of audited accounts for the past three years will help the case materially. Profit margins should not, in the absence of good cause, be forecast at a higher level than has previously been achieved; the size of the loan should not be overambitious and the need for it should be demonstrated to arise from expansionary trading objectives rather than some purely defensive cause.

5

Scrutinising the types and cost of funds

Profits are the rewards of success in business and are needed to provide:

1 The investor with a return for the use of the personal resources he has invested in the business, and
2 The company with an internal source of funds with which to expand

There are three broad types of sources of finance a company may have at its disposal:

1 Retained profits (including depreciation)
2 The more beneficial use of funds already deployed in the company
3 External funds

Retained profits

The commonest and most natural source of new funds for a company arises from that proportion of its annual after-tax profits which is not paid out by way of dividend. In fund terms, as was seen in Chapter 3, the amount of depreciation and amortisation should be added to the retained earnings in order to arrive at the cash flow.

It will be noted that the cash flow is not affected by the policy adopted by the directors on depreciation rates. A higher level of depreciation (a shorter period over which the cost is to be written off) would result in a correspondingly lower level of retained profit and vice versa. Since cash flow is based on the sum of the two, it is unaffected.

Dividend policy

On the other hand, it will be noted that the cash flow is directly affected by the policy adopted by the directors on dividends. Some parts of the share-capital structure (eg preference shares) leave the directors with no choice but to pay the required rate (unless insufficient profits have been earned or accumulated from previous years).

No ordinary shareholder, whether at a formal meeting or not, can require the company to pay a higher dividend than the directors recommend be paid. Often, therefore, directors have a conflict of interests over dividend policy. The company, with the management of which they have been entrusted, would prefer, on liquidity considerations, to pay a low rate of dividend or even none at all. On the other hand, the directors know that both the company's long-term interests (as well as their own employment) depends upon maintaining a good record as an investment.

Quoted companies, whose shares are dealt in on the Stock Exchange, have very different considerations from companies which may be owned by one man or a family. On the whole, such family businesses (some are very large and, until a few years ago, included such well-known names as the Sainsbury chain and Pilkington Glass) are more concerned with building up the value of their shares. Realised capital profits are subject only to 30 per cent capital gains tax, whereas receiving large dividends can result in the shareholder having to pay up to 98 per cent away in taxes.

Waiving dividends

It used to be quite common for the controlling shareholders, if they were few in number, to waive all or a part of their dividends with a view (*a*) to avoiding excessive personal tax and (*b*) to improving the company's liquidity and, thereby, increasing the chances of its more rapid expansion.

It is important to realise that these arrangements are now less simple than they were before the advent of capital transfer tax. Since this tax is leviable on the basis of 'loss to the donor' (rather than on the benefit to the donee), someone now waiving a dividend will, under certain circumstances, be held to have parted with a portion of the value of his shares — (Finance Act 1976).

More profitable use of existing funds

It is most likely that if a board of directors had the chance to set up their company from scratch again, they would arrange many, if not most, things differently. They might, for instance, decide that there was no need to have department A, or to cover territory B; the property at C was unnecessarily large; product D did not justify the cost of the stock levels which had to be maintained, etc, etc.

Need to study the overall position

What so many managements fail to appreciate is that most, if not all, of these types of change can be made without the mystical 'chance to start again'. Too many managements, particularly of the smaller and medium-sized companies, believe themselves to be so overworked that they claim not to have the time in which to rationalise. In no area is taking a step back, in order to study the overall position, more likely to yield positive and relatively quick results than in the financial area — and this is particularly so against a background of high inflation and ever increasing demands for borrowings.

Every company's resources are limited, but what there is available needs to be made the most of. In the next chapter there are considered the principal methods whereby a proportion of the funds already invested in a company can be released with the twin objectives of:

1 Deploying those funds more profitably and
2 Reducing the company's need for introducing further external funds to cover any unavoidable higher investment requirements (eg in stocks on account of inflation)

Short-term funds

The next part of this chapter considers the various forms of external finance which may be available to a company.

There is a general shortage of sound propositions being submitted to the financial institutions in these economically uncertain days. But if a business is sound, the management efficient and the product one with long-term marketability, there should be little problem in finding any necessary funds, albeit that a higher than normal proportion may have to come from overdraft and other short-term sources.

From the recipient's viewpoint, to have several offers and to be in a position to choose a financial partner is a state all too few companies enjoy. For, so often, companies delay the liquidity issue, which then has to be resolved in a hurry in a 'Hobson's choice' situation.

By 'short-term' is generally meant from 0 to 3 years. These forms of finance have varying effects upon the working capital of the company and, hence, upon the current ratio and quick ratio. The types of finance are:

1 Finance which affects current liabilities:
   (*a*) Bank overdrafts
   (*b*) Loans for 1 to 3 years
   (*c*) Suppliers' credit
   (*d*) Credit on taxes
   (*e*) Acceptance credits
   (*f*) Export finance
2 Finance which affects current assets:
   (*g*) Factoring
   (*h*) Invoice discounting

Bank overdrafts

These 'facilities' normally consist of an agreed credit limit on current account for up to one year. Overdrafts have the advantages of:

1 Cost — overdrafts are usually the cheapest of the many forms of loan finance a company can raise
2 Flexibility — the amount can be reduced, or increased up to the agreed limit, without notice, and the customer only pays interest on the actual amount which is borrowed on a day-to-day basis; also, the customer receives the benefit immediately of any reduction in borrowing rates and is free to substitute any other more attractive source of finance which presents itself
3 Being easy to arrange — compared with more permanent forms of finance, an overdraft is generally the least complicated to negotiate and quickest to have in use

Government 'squeezes'

The disadvantages of overdrafts, which include a sudden change of interest rates against the borrower, centre around the right of the facility to be terminated at short notice — technically, on demand. But provided whatever conditions were imposed on granting the facility are complied with, the term will generally be allowed to run its full course. Successive governments have used banking facilities as an easy form of control on the money supply; as a result, a company which relies too heavily on overdraft facilities can find itself very quickly and seriously affected in times of government 'squeezes'.

Banks do not consider it a part of their function to carry equity risks and the extent of their borrowing will depend on, among other things, the equity investment in the company. Nor do banks see it as their role to provide permanent capital; it is not uncommon today to find banks dividing the total agreed facility into the fixed and fluctuating parts, and requiring the former portion to be converted into a term loan bearing a higher rate of interest.

Bank overdrafts should be negotiated to meet:

1 General 'bridging' requirements pending more permanent sources of finance or the realising of unwanted assets
2 The difference between peak and minimum working-capital requirements over the year
3 Temporary increases in working capital (stocks) arising from a planned expansion of trade
4 Fluctuations within the month arising from cash receipts being bunched

The cost of an overdraft facility will vary depending upon the standing of the company, the security offered, the term required and, sometimes, the purpose for which the advance is needed. The usual interest rate is between 1 and 4 per cent above 'base rate', which moves in sympathy with, but not in direct ratio to, the minimum lending rate of the Bank of England.

Loans for 1 to 3 years

A term loan is made for a fixed period and carries interest either at a fixed rate for the whole period or, as is now more common, at a fixed percentage above one of the published 'base rates', eg the Finance Houses Association Base Rate. Such loans can be obtained from clearing banks, merchant banks and finance houses.

The cost of a fixed-rate term loan depends on the view taken by the institutions of the likely trend of interest rates generally. Short-term loans should be expected to cost between 2 and 5 per cent more than a normal overdraft. A variable-rate term loan may cost only 1 per cent more.

Suppliers' credit

Up to the period specified in their terms and conditions of sale, the credit granted by suppliers is both the cheapest and most readily available form of finance for a company. The cost is free unless either (*a*) it has been mutually agreed that interest will be payable after a particular period or (*b*) discounts receivable are lost by failure to pay accounts by their due dates.

It is important to realise what the cost is of a lost discount. For example, if on an invoice for £1000, 2½ per cent is offered for payment within 30 days, the cost of paying the invoice 1 week late is:

$$\frac{2.5}{100} \times £1000 = £25$$

This is an effective 130 per cent a year rate of interest:

$$\frac{£25}{£1000} \times \frac{365}{7} = 130\%$$

Subject to not antagonising the company's creditors to the point of losing their support, as much credit as possible should be taken once the discount period has been passed. In the example given above, it is worth noting that 92 days of credit (30 + 62) would need to be taken, once the discount had been lost, for the cost of this loss to cover the cost of borrowing the equivalent sum on overdraft at an assumed 15 per cent rate of interest because 62 days' credit at 15 per cent a year on £975 (£1000 less the 2½ per cent discount) would cost £25.

All other considerations apart, therefore, a company offered these terms should take one of two courses:

1 It should pay the account just in time to obtain the 2½ per cent discount, thereby gaining 30 days' free finance; or
2 It should pay the account later than 92 days, thereby gaining free credit to a value in excess of the cost of the lost discount

To pay the account on a date between the 30th and 92nd days would be to incur unnecessary expense.

Credit on taxes payable

The Revenue permit a free period of credit on most forms of tax, first between the date the liability arises and the date the tax is deemed payable and, secondly (but this concession is now severely restricted), between the date it is deemed payable and a later date by which, if the tax has been paid, no interest will become chargeable.

For example, corporation tax is payable by a company on a date between 9 and 23 months after the end of its financial year (the exact date depends on when the company used to pay its Schedule D tax prior to the introduction of corporation tax). Two further months of free credit used then to be permitted without an interest charge being incurred, but the Finance (No. 2) Act 1975 tightened the rules significantly for the payment of tax assessments made on or after 1 August 1975. Corporation tax liabilities now carry interest from 'the reckonable date' until payment is made. In most cases this 'reckonable date' is the later of (*a*) the date the tax is normally due and (*b*) 30 days after the assessment is made.

Interest on overdue taxes is not itself 'tax deductible'. The current rate of such interest is 9 per cent which, taking corporation tax at 52 per cent, is equivalent to paying a normal tax-deductible form of interest at 18.75 per cent. Therefore, unless overdraft interest rates exceed 18.75 per cent, it would pay the company to discharge its tax liabilities before, but only just before, the date on which interest would become chargeable.

The Revenue's attitude to PAYE tax payable by a company is somewhat different. They regard the company as being, in effect, temporary trustees of cash which *has already* been paid by employees and *is already* the property of the Revenue. PAYE is normally payable to the Revenue by the 19th day of the month following the one in which it is deductible from staff pay. If it is not so paid, the appropriate tax collection office will usually take steps within a matter of weeks to recover the debt.

It will be noted that by paying monthly salaries up to a date early in the month, instead of up to the last day of the previous month, almost an extra month's free credit on PAYE can be obtained.

VAT has yet to awaken the same degree of urgency at the Revenue. Although a company is, in effect, acting as the Revenue's collecting agent, there are no provisions for charging the company interest on its overdue payments. Indeed, the chasing-up procedures are such as to encourage companies to withhold payment for at least one or two months each quarter. Until such times as these procedures are tightened, every company which produces net output liabilities on VAT can make use of the interest-free facilities without penalty.

Acceptance credits

Acceptance credits are an alternative to normal overdraft facilities, and are mostly covered by either specific debts or identifiable goods (usually commodities).

Bills of exchange are drawn, generally for 60, 90 or 120 days, after which 'acceptance' is arranged by a bank or other institution of good standing in return for a commission; thereafter, on the strength of the acceptance house's guarantee to meet the bill on its due date in the event of the customer company defaulting, arrangements are made to 'discount' (sell) the bill for immediate cash. The price the company obtains reflects the cost to the purchasers of advancing the cash 60, 90 or 120 days before they, in turn, receive payment.

Today, it is possible and convenient for companies to raise three-month and shorter-term finance by drawing general bills (ie not against specific sale transactions) and to discount these, often at less cost than raising an equivalent temporary extra overdraft, through one of a number of reputable banks which handle such business.

There are three practical differences between a bill and an overdraft from the company's viewpoint:

1 A bill is less flexible than an overdraft and cannot, without penalty, be repaid either earlier or later than the date prescribed
2 A bill takes several days to arrange, whereas an overdraft facility, once negotiated, is available for immediate use
3 A bill is generally slightly more costly in interest terms than an overdraft; the interest is payable in advance, by deduction from the cash sum paid, and is at a fixed rate for the period

Export finance

The ECGD (Export Credits Guarantee Department) offers a form of insurance which enables exporting companies to obtain advances on preferential terms from clearing banks and certain other institutions (generally at ½ to 1 per cent *above* base rate) against overseas customers' debts awaiting payment.

Little publicity seems to be given to a more advantageous scheme for financing exports where the individual transactions are of at least a modest size. Under this scheme, the cost in interest terms can be several points *below* base rate. UK clearing banks seem reluctant to alert their customers to these more favourable facilities, under which loans not exceeding six months are arranged in one or other of the 'strong' currencies. Besides the exceptionally low rates of interest payable, complete protection is afforded against changes in currency exchange rates during the period of such loans.

Factoring

Three general points should be drawn to the reader's attention about both factoring and invoice discounting before distinguishing the two:

1 There are a very large number of relatively minor variations to the basic legal relationships, to the methods of trading and to the administrative requirements of the companies which offer these services. Accordingly, the broad descriptions, given below, of each

form of finance will not necessarily fit in precisely with readers' own experiences in this field

2 There are a few companies which purport to offer such services, at least by name, whose methods both from the legal aspect and administratively, leave their 'clients' very vulnerable financially, and under permanent threat of a total breakdown to their customer relations. The most exhaustive enquiry is recommended before a contract is signed with any organisation

3 Trade debts which have already been charged to a debenture cannot be used to raise finance by either of these methods without the consent of those debenture holders. (It is common for a bank overdraft to be secured by a floating debenture on, among other things, the debts of the company.)

Factoring, and to a lesser extent invoice discounting, is much on the increase, and no company, however large, should now feel it would be losing status for it to become known it was factoring its debts. Provided it contracts with one of the large financial operators of sound repute, it will find itself in both good hands and distinguished company.

When a company 'factors' its debts, administratively it hands over the entire running of its sales ledger to the factoring company. The latter determines each customer's credit limit, it issues the statements, it collects the cash and often supplies sales and other statistics to the client company. The factoring company generally takes either an equitable or legal assignment of the debts, effectively guaranteeing the debts. In practice, companies sometimes require higher credit limits for certain of their customers than the factoring company is prepared to agree to, in which case the company has to provide 'recourse' in the event of non-payment.

There are two distinct parts to the operation with the factoring company. The first, the administrative service described in the previous paragraph, is undertaken for an agreed fee, usually calculated at between 1 and 2½ per cent of the company's turnover (the average invoice value and number of credit notes issued have a significant bearing on this cost). The average period of credit is determined from past records and agreed between the parties — say 90 days. The factor then undertakes to pay to the company, 90 days after each invoice it issues (a copy is sent to the factoring company for book-keeping purposes), its full value whether or not the factoring company itself has received payment.

The second part of the operation is a loan facility (this may not be taken up by companies without liquidity problems which only seek a sales ledger service); under this, an advance is made by the factoring company generally equal to 80 per cent of the debts currently outstanding. This advance, for which the interest charge is usually between 2 and 4 per cent above base rate, is 'topped up', usually once or twice a week, so as to equal the 80 per cent after taking into account the amounts anyway payable to the company by way of the 90-day period having expired on earlier debts.

Invoice discounting

Under an invoice discounting arrangement, the company continues to run its own sales ledger and accepts sole responsibility for the collection of its debts; also, any bad debts which may arise. Unlike when a factoring service is employed, the company's customers need never know that it is using the service.

On the strength of the company's balance sheet generally, the invoice-discounting company offers a facility up to an agreed limit. To obtain temporary advances within the prescribed sum, the company must assign batches of invoices (the debts thereby created) to the finance company which, on receipt, will advance a prescribed percentage of the total value, usually 70 per cent. It will be noted that not all invoices have to be discounted, nor does the facility have to be used all the year round.

Such temporary advances have to be repaid when:

1 The debtor pays his account; or
2 The prescribed normal credit period expires

whichever happens first. If the normal credit period expires first then the company has to find the necessary funds from its own resources — or from discounting new invoices.

Custom varies between the many finance companies offering this service, but most will not advance a sum which exceeds 50 per cent of the current total debtor value of the company. The total potential facility is, therefore, smaller than that available from a full factoring service; the interest charges on the advances are the same.

Medium-term funds

By 'medium-term' is generally meant from three to a maximum of ten years.

Hire-purchase finance
It is usual to consider under this term certain arrangements for acquiring the use of fixed assets which do not strictly involve either the purchase of the asset or, therefore, the funding of an acquisition cost. Hire-purchase transactions are an obvious example under which, legally, the asset does not become the property of the company until the end of the contractual hire period; it is then usual to pass ownership for a nominal consideration.

Hire-purchase is a considerably more common form of finance today even with large companies and has many advantages. It is easy to arrange; it does not disturb other sources of finance which may have resulted in fully owned assets being charged as security. Hire-purchase does not normally enter into 'borrowing-limit' considerations, and it has no inherent tax disadvantages.

There are many companies of sound repute which offer industrial hire-purchase and, though companies which also have a domestic side to their business tend to offer less attractive terms, it is possible to find organisations offering five years' hire-purchase with a variable interest rate as low as 2½ per cent above Finance House Base Rate. A deposit is required (usually about 15 per cent) but much of this can be recovered quite quickly if the company is one which can recover its input VAT (included by the HP company in the total figure it is financing).

By acquiring an asset on hire-purchase, a company will, under current legislation, lose neither the 100 per cent writing-down allowance for tax, nor any grants it qualifies for. The interest paid is tax-deductible on business assets.

Leasing finance
Leasing finance, with a secured contractual obligation, is another form of finance which is generally considered under the medium-term, but leasing, which was popular before the advent of the 100 per cent writing-down allowance, now has serious tax disadvantages. The finance company, unlike in a transaction involving hire-purchase, is itself given the tax allowances and any grant which the equipment qualifies for; it should allow for these benefits in the hire charge it levies. However, that hire charge, which is a tax-deductible item for the hiring company, is spread evenly over the period, perhaps five years, thereby deferring the full benefits of the tax allowances and grants.

Other forms of medium-term finance include 'term loans' of the kind described under the previous section, but naturally of longer duration. Generally, the longer the period the higher will be the interest rate if this is on a fixed-rate basis.

If interest rates are low, in one of the cyclical troughs which occur, and a reasonable fixed rate can be negotiated, other considerations apart, a company should arrange a longer rather than shorter term. But if the loan has to be taken up at a time when interest rates are high, then it is often better to opt for a short-term commitment. However, a company can never be assured that a short-term facility will be renewed and, as has already been pointed out, it is important for it to finance the greater part of its overall requirements from long-term sources.

Medium-term loans are generally obtained from banks and merchant banks and, except for quoted companies, are often accompanied by the issue of a modest slice of equity.

Interest 'cover'

The profit's cover for loan interest has been referred to already, with a 4 or 5 times cover being considered necessary by most would-be lenders. There is, however, another type of cover; this quantifies the company's ability to make sufficient profit retentions in order to be able to redeem the loan when it falls to be repaid.

Say a five-year loan is being contemplated. If it is considered unlikely that this could be repaid at the end, except out of another loan arranged for that purpose, then it may be necessary to consider either a loan of greater duration or raising part of the funds by way of new shares. Consider Figure 5:1, which shows that company A would be unable to redeem its loan of £700,000 without recourse to a form of substitute finance (termed 're-funding') when the time arrived.

In practice, today, few companies which are not obligated to do so by their loan agreements are creating sinking funds. This is simply because they require to use such funds within the company to keep pace with inflation. They are relying on being able to make alternative arrangements (eg a substitute loan) when their present debt falls due for redemption.

Long-term funds

By 'long-term' is generally meant from 10 years upwards. The main sources are the insurance companies and pension schemes which, because of their special tax status, can be interested by rates of return which would not be acceptable to sources of shorter-term loans.

Security is the major consideration, and probably the most common arrangement is for one of the company's properties to be mortgaged.

This form of finance is also often used as a means of raising funds for the erection of new factories and offices.

Figure 5:1 Cover for redeeming a loan

	Company A	Company B
	£'000	£'000
Trading profit	500	1,000
Interest (say $14\frac{1}{4}$ per cent on £700,000)	100	100
Net profit before tax	400	900
Taxation (say 50%)	200	450
Available for dividend	200	450
Dividend (say 50% of surplus)	100	225
Retained earnings	100	225
Five years' retentions (assuming they are not otherwise required) ignoring appreciation in the value of any sinking fund itself over the period	500	1,125

Special facilities

Successive governments have encouraged capital investment, particularly in areas of high unemployment, by providing grants to help finance qualifying expenditure. Frequent amendments are made to the terms of these grants, including their rates, the geographical areas they cover and the types of expenditure they are meant to embrace. The initiative for claiming grants lies solely with the companies, which should take the required action at the earliest date possible. (For instance, certain types of expenditure on factory improvements will only qualify provided a detailed examination has been carried out by the appropriate authorities before any work is begun.)

Compared with tax allowances, from which companies only benefit when they have profits to set against them, grants are paid in cash (generally within about three months) irrespective of whether the company has reached the profitable stage in its development or not.

In certain 'Development Areas' of the country it is possible to obtain interest-free government loans (or ones carrying only a nominal rate of interest) for the purpose of financing the building of new factories, or extensions, when the result will provide new employment for more than a given number of workers.

Additionally, government assistance is available in activities of labour training, promoting exports and assisting specific types of industry. It is surprising how many companies are quite unaware of the facilities which they can obtain.

Providing the security

For a loan to be offered to a company, the lender must be sure that:

1 The money will be repaid by the company on the due date (ie the company will be able meanwhile to generate the necessary funds)
2 The agreed rate of interest will be paid during the currency of the loan (ie the company will earn sufficient pre-interest profits from which to be able to meet such interest)
3 The money will be repaid from some alternative source on the due date if the company fails in its obligations (ie the loan is adequately secured by guarantees and/or pledged 'securities' the sale of which could be enforced as a last resort)

A would-be lender will seek the maximum of security which can be negotiated above what is regarded as the acceptable minimum. The company, on the other hand, will want to part with the minimum, since to give security can:

1 Restrict the use of those assets (eg block the sale or alteration, or subleasing of a property)
2 Prevent those same assets being charged, except in subordination, as security on a further, perhaps more important, loan

Borrowing powers

Because there is a limit to what assets it can pledge as security, the borrowings of every company are limited. It is important to realise, also, that a company cannot provide security for borrowings contracted in excess of its own power to borrow (see Chapter 3), and if any security is so given it is void at law.

Where a loan is made to a company by a single party it is convenient to provide the security by way of mortgage. But where several parties are to provide the funds, each to have recourse to the same security, it is usual to issue debenture stock secured by a trust deed giving a charge on specified assets in favour of trustees.

The reader is referred to Chapter 3 where a summary of the main characteristics of debentures and other secured loans is given. It is common to find banks requiring a floating charge as security for an overdraft, and very often the terms of the facility provide that if the company later creates a fixed charge on any assets comprised within the floating charge, then the facility will become repayable immediately. The reason for this is that, at law, a fixed charge has priority over a floating charge.

Subject to any limitations imposed by its memorandum and articles of association, a company may charge any of its assets, present or future. It may also charge its uncalled capital.

It is a function of the board of directors to fund the company's debt at the lowest possible cost which is consistent with an acceptable level of risk.

Permanent new share capital

This book is concerned primarily with the internal management of a company's finances. Advanced academic considerations on 'lowest acceptable rates of return' and 'risk analysis' on raising cash from the general public are unlikely to be within the control function of many company readers, and are not examined in detail.

If a company is expanding, or is planned to expand, at a rate which is beyond the capacity of its retained earnings and short-term loans to finance, it is necessary to raise additional long-term capital. This capital can be in the form of either shares or debt.

New share capital, either in the form of equity or carrying preferred rights, is needed in two basic situations:

1 To preserve the gearing — the ratio between share capital and debt
2 To provide a wider base on the strength of which the company will be enabled to increase its short-term and other borrowings

If the requirement for extra capital is large in proportion to the size of the company, it is probable that, in practice, a part will have to be raised by the issue of new equity shares. This is becoming an increasingly common requirement with institutional lenders, who seek a 'share of the cake' in addition to the simple reward of interest on any loan.

Comparison between preference shares and debt

The issue of new preference shares has become an event of the past. Dividend rates have moved well ahead of the 5, 6 and 7½ per cent rates which were common and are still seen in the share structure of older companies.

New preference shares are now unpopular with private investors and companies alike. For the investors, even if carrying dividends of 10 per cent or higher, they do not offer the same proof against inflation which, it is claimed, ordinary shares do. For the company, not being a tax-deductible item of expense, a preference dividend effectively costs a company more than the equivalent interest charge on debt, as is shown in Figure 5:2.

Figure 5:2 Franked and unfranked income

	Preference shares £'000	Debt £'000
Trading profit	1,000	1,000
Interest charge	—	200
Net profit before tax	1,000	800
Taxation at 52%	520	416
Net profit after tax	480	384
Preference dividend	130 *	—
Available for ordinary shareholders	350	384

*Equivalent to the same gross amount as the interest charge on the debt — ie £200,000 less income tax at 35%

Preference and other dividends on shares are termed 'franked investment income' when received by a company resident in the United Kingdom, and entitle the recipient to have the tax credit paid to it if it is exempt from corporation tax. Preference shareholders, however, often include pension funds which can recover tax at the corporation-tax rate and are not advantaged to the same extent on any interest they receive.

This distinction is important if, as some companies have tried to do in order to gain a tax advantage for themselves, they seek to convert their preference shares into unsecured loan stock (carrying tax-deductible interest). If pension funds hold some of the preference shares, they are likely to oppose the move.

Mergers and takeovers

A consideration of alternative sources of finance would not be complete without a brief reference to merging with or selling out a controlling interest to another and, possibly, larger company which has either spare funds or the means of obtaining what is required.

Of the large number of amalgamations which are conducted every year, it is impossible to say how many really work out as planned. So often one or other management becomes disillusioned or frustrated, friction grows and the only solution to what is sometimes referred to as 'the chemistry problem' is for one party to move out altogether.

There is probably no such entity as the 'ideal partner', but a fair test of whether one has found a good one is to ask how often it has been necessary to refer back to the contracts by which the merger was originally brought to fruition. Continual quarreling over what one party did or did not undertake to do, will all too soon undermine authority and have far-reaching consequences on the morale of the senior staff.

The time to raise doubts about the outcome of a merger is before it is consummated: Are the other people with whom you will be working, people whom you can trust and people with whom you really do want to work?

The 'cost' of merging or agreeing to be taken over is not so much the pecuniary outlay (which can, incidently, be surprisingly high) as the loss of the value the vendors attach to being their own masters — or, at least, responsible to no one but their own shareholders. No two groups are run the same way and it is expecting a lot of an enterprising management, who are merely seeking further funds with which to expand, for them to have to conform with what appears at first sight to be 'a lot of head office bureaucracy'.

The backbone of British industry is made up of relatively small independent companies — there is much to be said for encouraging successful firms to retain that distinguished status.

6

Releasing inert funds and gaining credit

In the previous chapter, the many possible sources of finance available to a company, and their respective costs, were considered. In this chapter, it is proposed to offer readers the opportunity to question:

1 Whether their company's existing methods of funding are necessarily the most appropriate in today's special conditions, and
2 Whether their company's trading customs, purchasing procedures, tax planning etc are conducive to minimising any apparently unavoidable requirement for new external funds

(The same considerations should also be applied in situations where, for example, a bank is insisting that a company reduces its current overdraft.)

No management should seek additional funds from outside sources without first ensuring that there do not exist in the company already, funds which could be more profitably redeployed.

Such inert funds, which are almost always cheaper than negotiating new external sources, fall into the following categories to which, for convenience, has been added postponing payment of certain liabilities:

1 Funds invested in assets which are not necessary to the future prosperity of the company (eg an excess of stock)
2 Funds invested in assets which are capable of being turned directly into cash (eg debtors)
3 Funds invested in assets which, although they may be fully utilised, may be financed by other methods than using the company's own limited capital (eg property)

4 Liabilities, the payment of which can legitimately be deferred without cost (eg certain taxes)

Stocks

When scrutinising assets in order to reduce investment a large proportion of the time should be devoted to the item known as 'stock'.

The subject is a vast one, and cannot be dealt with more than cursorily in a book of this length and overall subject content. The best that can be done in this context, is to indicate the broad areas which should exercise the minds and the imagination of managements.

To set about the problem by cutting all stock by an arbitrary percentage is a not uncommon expedient, but one which rarely proves to be of any real value since as many new problems are usually created as are cured. The object may well be to cut the total stock level by, say, 10 per cent but the method must be scientifically founded with individual parts and lines of product receiving individual scrutiny.

In a manufacturing company, stock is held in three forms, namely raw materials, work-in-progress and finished goods. Retailers and wholesalers deal only in finished items except where their trade centres around the provision of materials (eg a builders' merchant). There cannot, therefore, be any universally accepted standard of what is the 'right' level of stocks which all companies should maintain or even what proportion of their capital should be locked up in this asset.

Conflicting divisional requirements

Each company's management should evaluate what is the optimum level needed to satisfy most nearly the three operating divisions involved and their conflicting interests.

These are:

1 The sales division, which would like to see maximum stock levels in order to be able to supply customers ex-stock (early delivery is a powerful factor in obtaining orders against competition)
2 The factory division, which would like a constant level of production all the year round and for this to be organised in long runs to minimise machine changes; also, high levels of raw materials to be maintained so production is never interrupted
3 The finance division, which would like to see minimum-sized orders for raw material (consistent with economical production runs) and for no finished goods to be stocked, all goods being delivered on

completion of manufacture

Stocks require to be controlled, not in total (though such statistics can be a useful pointer to adverse changes) but item by item. Reordering for the maintenance of optimum stock levels should be based upon ensuring:

1 Sufficient stocks are carried to meet customers' normal requirements
2 Levels of finished goods and work-in-progress do not exceed the requirements for the expected level of sales during the period it would take to manufacture replacement stocks
3 Production runs need to be for specified minimum quantities, to be economical

Cost of holding stock

Stock not only calls for the investment of substantial parts of a company's capital, it also incurs many running costs during its transitory ownership by the company:

1 The cost of the finance invested in it
2 The cost of storing it, which includes warehousing, racking and bins, insurance, heat and light, security, handling equipment and all necessary staff
3 The cost of lost and damaged items, obsolescence and losses in value due to fashion changes

Examination and analysis

Management should set about the reduction of stock levels by instituting a campaign of examination and analysis, the main areas of which might be:

1 Analyse the stock records and examine the stock with a view to disposing of all obsolete and damaged items
2 Analyse the form the continuous audit checks take. For financial accounting purposes it is necessary to know that *x* number of a certain part should be in stock and were found to be in stock; for liquidity purposes 'movements' are more relevant, it being necessary to know how many of those parts were actually used in, say, one month and to question whether that part could be discontinued and another, already in wider use, be substituted. Important lines of stock should have age analyses carried out, as is done in the case of debtors

3 Analyse stock levels by location — are too many 'dumps' of similar stock items being permitted, each with its own minimum level?
4 Analyse how often stockout situations do actually arise (do not rely on warehousemen's memories, examine the facts). Analyse the degree of importance if certain lines do go out of stock. Is production affected, or can another similar part be used? As regards finished stock, is the sales division insisting on an unnecessarily high standard of supply?
5 Analyse in a manufacturing situation the cost of more frequent changeovers in plant (these usually involve extra unproductive setting-up times). It may be found that to double the frequency of changeovers, with halved batch quantities, will enable the stock level also to be halved
6 Analyse the gross contribution on each product. How many products, when all oncosts (sales, administrative and delivery overheads, and finance charges whilst in stock) have been taken into account, yield no profit? What would be the effect on the company's business if such products were eliminated altogether from its range?
7 Analyse the effects of shortening a long manufacturing cycle, which causes a heavy investment in work-in-progress, by increasing the production capacity. It may be possible to fill any resulting overcapacity by undertaking subcontracting work which does not involve so high a working-capital investment. Alternatively, analyse the effects of terminating certain processes and buying partly processed components instead
8 Analyse the level of work-in-progress which arises because of delays between processes. Can the production cycle be better organised so as to reduce the time between the start of manufacture and the final emergence of the finished product?
9 Analyse the current lead times on all deliveries, and enquire if favourable changes are always given effect to by lowering reorder levels

How much ready cash?

Solvency can be assured by holding large amounts of cash, but 'cash in hand and at bank' is part of a company's working capital which, in turn, is financed from long-term sources. To hold an excessive balance of cash therefore becomes expensive. Furthermore, it is unnecessary if the management is effective, which means it is planning an optimum course, neither wasting its liquid funds nor running undue risk of becoming technically insolvent.

A company which is experiencing liquidity problems all the year round is more likely to be operating an overdraft rather than being in possession of a credit balance at the bank. But some seasonal businesses, at some times of the year, find themselves with spare funds.

Ready cash in the form of notes and coins on a company's premises should, for security reasons, be kept to an absolute minimum. Cash drawings for wages are usually made weekly, at which time petty cash floats are also topped up. Wages drawings should, if possible, not be made before the day on which they are actually used.

Money has to be put to use to make profits; ready cash in the form of a credit balance on current account represents idle funds earning no reward. The overall objective of cash planning must be to use all temporary liquid resources a company finds itself with, and to use them in such a form that, if circumstances suddenly change, they can quickly be turned back into cash.

It seldom pays to place surplus funds on a local bank's seven-day deposit account (rates of interest several per cent higher are normally obtainable through the bank's head office), though this is convenient if the amounts are small and the period short (large sums, even if only available for 24 hours, can be invested profitably on the money market for the 'overnight' rate of interest).

Longer-term funds, if they cannot be more profitably used in the company, can be invested in government dated stocks. A stock with a high or low coupon may be chosen; the capital value of the low-coupon stock is likely to appreciate more than the higher one (except at times of a major decrease in interest rates generally) and, if the stock can be held for a clear twelve months, any capital profit then realised will be tax-free.

Local authorities offer attractive rates of interest, generally for deposits of 1, 3, 6 or 12 months; most carry government backing as security. Treasury bills not only carry good rates of interest, but can be easily sold before maturity if the cash is required earlier than was envisaged.

Banking procedures

All companies, particularly those experiencing liquidity problems, should bank all cash and cheques on the day they are received. Whenever possible this banking should be at the branch where the company's account is kept. Valuable credit may be lost if cheques are paid into a convenient local branch from where a credit slip has then to be posted, or sent through some central bank clearing, to the branch which maintains the account. This basic rule should override all other considerations, such as may happen, for example, when a bank manager who has known the account for a long period, moves to another area and the directors want to move the account with him.

If a company with a £5,000,000 turnover delays by an average of four days the crediting of receipts to its current account on which there is an overdraft, that overdraft will, on average:

1 Be £55,000 higher than it need be (effectively reducing the limit agreed with the bank by the same amount) and
2 Cost the company £8,200 per year unnecessarily (on the assumption it is paying interest at 15 per cent a year)

Setoff arrangements
No company should operate more than one bank current account unless it has an agreed 'offset' arrangement with the bank. Under this, the balances on all the accounts, whether debit or in credit, will be netted off to one figure each day for the purpose of calculating any interest charge which may be payable. It is practical for most groups of companies (certainly in respect of wholly owned subsidiaries) to operate offset arrangements also, thereby minimising either interest charges or the frequent need to be passing cheques from one account to another.

Many companies pay their monthly salaries by the credit transfer method; this avoids the administrative burden of drawing and issuing individual cheques, but does result in the company's bank account being debited with the total cost up to 2 weeks before the equivalent cheques would be presented (instructions for credit transfers generally have to reach the bank, which debits the cost immediately, at a minimum of 5 days before the month end).

Sacred cows

A comprehensive assessment of funds invested in assets which may not be necessary to the future prosperity of the company would, in most companies, be likely to redden a few faces. The failed projects, for example which should, perhaps, never have been begun and have just been kept going.

In general, the same economic examination should periodically be given to continuing with what were once examined as 'new projects' as was given in deciding to begin them. Great difficulties can be encountered in getting managements to acknowledge that they made mistakes in the first place. In consequence, unprofitable ventures are sometimes carried on *ad infinitum*. When liquidity is short, it is invariably better to cut the losses and concentrate all a company's skills and financial resources on the areas which unquestionably yield the best results.

Other examples of sacred cows, which can represent unnecessary investments are: penthouses, ostensibly used for essential company entertaining; pretentious motor cars; ostentatious furniture and fittings in executives' offices — sometimes also in their secretaries' offices (part of the status game); the managing director's secretary who, herself, engages a secretary 'to do the typing'. The justification for maintaining such levels of luxury should be assessed in the light of each company's general prosperity and liquidity position.

Trade investments

Many companies, particularly small and medium-sized ones, feature on their balance sheets a heading: 'trade investments'. This represents the cost of various shares which have been acquired over the years in companies with which there might, at one time, have been relatively close personal links. For example, a company might have bought some shares in one of its principal suppliers or customers.

Unquoted shares comprising minority holdings in small companies are unlikely to be other than ignored as a form of security by would-be lenders to the company.

When a company is experiencing liquidity problems it should examine the justification for retaining any of these holdings. It should question whether the preferential arrangements, which were once associated with a particular shareholding, are still of some consequence. On the economics side, the dividends being earned are probably small.

Debtors

The amount of credit offered to customers and the amount taken by them today are usually at two very different levels. If it is the custom of the trade to give credit, then it is a foolish management which refuses to offer similar terms to those of its competitors and permit a small degree of toleration. But they must get tough with persisent defaulters.

In the previous chapter, factoring arrangements were explained and it was pointed out that many companies are turning to this service, which embraces one very important area of responsibility — credit control. Factoring is a relatively convenient, and by no means costly method of raising finance, and at the same time unburdens the company of the ever-increasing cost of running its own sales ledger.

The credit controller

If a company in a credit-giving trade is not prepared to factor its debts, then it is essential for it to have a highly efficient sales ledger section. Credit controllers have gained in status over recent years as companies have come to depend more upon the earliest possible collection of their cash receipts.

A credit controller functions in two areas:

1 He fixes credit limits based on his assessment of the risk involved with each customer; he should be continually up-dating his assessments in the light of published and other information which comes to his notice. He should not adopt so cautious an approach as to stifle growth, on the other hand, he must refuse credit when he has information to think the risk is unduly high
2 He is responsible for maintaining the sales ledger and for collecting the debts within the credit period agreed

The procedures employed in many companies are not conducive to the earliest receipt of cash. For example, delays are experienced even at the first step — the issue of invoices. Normally a debt arises at the time goods are despatched. Invoices should be dated accordingly and themselves despatched without delay (many companies process the invoices they receive for payment without reference to suppliers' statements).

On the other hand, statements are the medium by which many companies do draw their monthly cheques, and these should be despatched within a few days of the end of a month, even at the cost of omitting an invoice for goods sent on the last day or two of the month.

Where it is practicable for the company, and its customers can be persuaded to agree, direct-debit methods of collection offer such benefits that consideration should be given to offering a special cash incentive.

Cost of a bad debt

A bad debt is more than a loss of gross contribution — it is a straight loss of profit comprised of (*a*) cost of stock, (*b*) gross margin and (*c*) if applicable, VAT calculated on the selling price. (VAT cannot be reclaimed on bad debts, but depending upon the circumstances, it is sometimes possible to issue a credit note.)

There are other means by which companies can lessen their investment in debtors:

1 Increase the 'minimum-order' level — companies are often better profitwise, as well as in liquidity terms, if small orders (which generally incur a disproportionate level of handling and administrative costs) are not accepted. Customers who order in small quantities often prove to be the slowest payers
2 Ensure that larger orders do not become small despatches and small-amount invoices. The procedure for handling orders which cannot immediately be entirely satisfied from stock, should be examined
3 Prevent salesmen receiving too high a proportion of their total remuneration by way of commission (which leads to a 'Got to sell to live' attitude developing and the taking of orders from customers they know, at best, will be very slow payers). Commissions are often cancelled when bad debts arise; it is the persistent slow payer who also needs to be struck from the customer list
4 Offer discounts for prompt payment. Today, with high interest rates and liquidity problems common, this form of inducement can have two disadvantages. First, the discount has to be quite high to have any effect and, second, many customers will take the discount even though the stated credit period has been exceeded
5 Review the policy on giving trade discounts. Because they have done so for a great many years, some companies are continuing, in times of very changed circumstances, to offer trade discounts to outlets which, in reality, have no right to expect privileged terms
6 Telephone the boss. Numerous books have been written on the art of how to get the cash in, and readers who believe their 'dunning letter' methods are ineffective should experiment with direct telephoning techniques on the larger debts. For example, a girl with a pleasing manner who is prepared to use a bit of cunning, can produce some quick responses. Such tricks as telephoning the managing director, not revealing her own company's name but saying it is a 'personal call', may not sound especially businesslike — but nor is the customer's inexcusable delay in meeting its financial obligations especially businesslike

Freehold Property

Clearly, if any freehold property is not required for the company's current or foreseeable operations, it should be disposed of. Timing is important since the industrial and office property market is cyclical by nature. Properties which are too large should have any unused areas sublet.

If its freehold property is essential to a company with a severe liquidity problem, two broad alternatives are available:

1 To raise a mortgage on the security of the property. Generally, mortgage loans equal to about 70 per cent of the current market value of the property can be obtained from pension funds and insurance companies on reasonably attractive terms
2 To arrange a 'sale and leaseback'. Under this form of transaction the property is sold but simultaneously leased back from the purchaser. The company remains in occupation and in future pays a rent on what has become only a leasehold interest

Subject to finding a buyer for the property who is prepared to pay its full market value the company will realise immediately about 40 to 45 per cent more cash under a sale and leaseback than by merely raising a loan.

Sale and leaseback

There are, however, five main drawbacks to sale and leaseback:

1 New leases invariably contain seven-year review clauses under which the tenant becomes liable to pay progressively higher rents, such amounts not being fixed until near each review date
2 Depending upon the terms of the lease, on its termination, the tenant may face a substantial liability for dilapidations
3 The taxation implications of all sale and leaseback transactions need particularly careful study. (Following a number of notable abuses by 'property developers' some years ago, legislation was introduced which also caught some quite innocent transactions in its net)
4 The company is selling its long-term interests in the property outright, thereby disposing for ever of the opportunity to partake in any future appreciation in its value
5 The last disadvantage in some cases virtually negatives the aim to improve liquidity. A bank agrees to an overdraft facility on the strength of a company's balance sheet. Even if the bank does not take

a fixed charge on the company's property, it may take a floating charge or it may only assess the realisable value and take an overall view of the security afforded. If the company then disposes of a property — possibly the main security in the eyes of the bank — in order, perhaps, to pay off its pressing creditors and invest more heavily in stocks, a completely new set of facts face the bank. It is probable in such circumstances that the bank would seek to withdraw, or at least reduce, the borrowing facility

Managements with liquidity problems and saleable properties on their balance sheets should not overlook the financial advantages of moving the whole company to a Development Area, where government grants are offered on new factories and certain classes of labour.

Leasehold property

Almost all the points raised under the previous section are equally applicable to leasehold interests in property. It is even possible to 'sale and lease back' some properties which are already on lease. In this instance what is being sold is the capital value of the 'profit rental'. A company may have enjoyed for many years the benefit of a long lease under terms which do not reflect the current level of rents. It is possible, if the period until the original lease falls in is long enough, to sell this 'head lease' for a capital sum and to enter into a new lease with the purchaser at a rent which does reflect current levels.

Plant and machinery

It is not generally practical to 'sale and lease back' items of plant, and industrial hire-purchase is rarely available on secondhand equipment.

However, since a portion of the old items of plant are almost continuously being retired and replacements purchased, the main opportunity for releasing funds under this heading lies in:

1 Selling off scrapped and obsolete equipment; and
2 Acquiring the replacements under hire-purchase

Long-term leasing is not, generally, advocated today for the reasons outlined in the previous chapter. However, a large amount of 'plant hire', which is short-term in character, is undertaken. To hire expensive plant as and when it is needed, as opposed to buying it and then not using it for long periods, makes financial sense in these days of illiquidity, quicker obsolesence and high maintenance charges.

Motor vehicles

As in the case of plant, motor vehicles are being sold and replaced almost as a continual process. Vehicles can be hire-purchased, but the arrangements available are an adjunct to the domestic market and tend to be costly for companies.

'Contract hire' is now a quite common form of financing fleets of cars, vans or lorries. The parameters of the contract vary from hire company to hire company, but usually the basic charge covers all maintenance, replacement vehicles in the event of breakdown and depreciation up to a stated mileage. Insurance charges are sometimes also included. The hirer pays for petrol and oil.

Any quotation for contract hire should be carefully compared with the company's costs of owning and maintaining its own fleet. Such costs should of course, take account of the cost of the finance tied up in the written-down value of the vehicles. It will generally be found that, economically, contract hire will only be justified on paper if it can result in staff and administrative savings within the company. If the company is small, and organising its own fleet is one of several responsibilities of one man, no saving of his costs is likely to arise from the change. But as a means of freeing funds for more profitable use, contract hire should be considered as possibly justifying the marginally higher running cost.

Taxation

Taking credit on liabilities for taxation was considered in the previous chapter. It is, however, possible to improve the overall tax position even further, and quite legally.

For example, in a group some of the more recently formed companies probably have to pay their corporation tax nine months after their year-end, whereas many of the longer-established companies are allowed up to 23 months. In these circumstances, tax can be further deferred (by up to 14 months) by passing profits from the newer companies over to the older ones by way of, for example, 'management charges' (assuming the relevant companies are wholly owned). These so-called 'end-of-year adjustments' need not affect the management accounting or the results upon which local managers are judged; they are adjustments to the financial accounts only.

It follows that any new ventures, diversifications etc, which the management choose to operate through new companies should have their profits absorbed into companies with later pay dates for tax.

Trading losses
Companies which incur losses should receive from other companies in the same group, management charges or 'contributions' towards their outgoings, as year-end adjustments; these should come, as far as is practicable, from profitable companies which have early tax-payment dates. Some groups elect to be taxed on a group basis, when such losses will be automatically offset against the total of profits.

A further area for deferring tax may arise in companies with a distinctly seasonal trade. They should choose a year-end date just prior to the sales peak; if this is done, the resulting profit will not be taxed until the following year.

Groups with overseas companies are enabled sometimes to take advantage of lower rates of taxation on 'unremitted' profits.

Corporation-tax assessments can be reduced through the careful classification of certain items of capital expenditure. For example, the cost of any electrical and plumbing fittings and fire sprinklers should be added to 'plant and machinery', which qualifies for 100 per cent writing-down allowances in the first year, and not to the property account.

Most interest charges arising on loans are deductible in assessing a company's liability to corporation tax, not on an 'accruals basis' (as the cost will appear in the financial accounts), but on a 'cash-payments' basis. Accordingly, it is beneficial to arrange for interest payments on new loans to fall due just prior to the company's year-end rather than shortly afterwards.

Dividends

Preference-share dividends are generally payable on prescribed dates and should be so paid. As far as is practicable, the payment of ordinary dividends should be set at as late a date as possible in a company's financial year.

There is considerable room for manoeuvring the payment of the ACT (advance corporation tax) liability, which is currently equal to 35/65ths (about 54 per cent) of the dividend itself and was as high as almost 74 per cent during 1974/75.

ACT is broadly equivalent to the tax which used to be deducted by companies when dividends were declared gross. Since the introduction of the imputation system of company taxation, dividends have been declared net, but the company has still to pay over to the Revenue the equivalent of the tax credit. (This tax is treated as an advance payment towards the company's eventual 'mainstream' corporation tax.) ACT is payable to the Revenue within 14 days of the end of the 'return period' during which a 'relevant distribution' is made; these return periods run for three months (except for the quarter which includes the company's year-end) and it follows that the payment of ACT can be deferred by up to almost three months by deferring the payment of an ordinary dividend to the beginning of the next return period.

Since, however, ACT is treated as an advance payment of corporation tax in respect of whichever year the dividend is actually paid in, it follows that it is beneficial to pay a year-end dividend just prior to, rather than just after the year-end date. This enables the ACT credit to be taken one year earlier.

Creditors

The only possible 'inert funds' falling under this heading lie in paying trade and expense creditors before what can best be described as 'the latest practicable date'. No one should advocate a policy of virtually waiting to be sued, because it certainly does not help a company's reputation for it to become known as a slow payer.

On the other hand, there are private companies where the quill-pen age has not died and outstanding creditors are religiously paid on the last day of each month 'because they always have been'.

As is more fully described in Chapter 13, the drawing of cheques should be scheduled month by month, if not weekly, with a view to seeing when it may be beneficial to take cash discounts and by what date it is essential to pay important suppliers if future supplies are not to be jeopardised. Certain expense creditors do not press for payment for several months (for example local-authority rates), and such outgoings should be scheduled accordingly.

Purchasing and overheads

The activities of both purchasing and selling have a major influence on a company's liquidity — purchasing from the viewpoint of (*a*) buying good value and avoiding waste, thereby directly saving on expenditure, and (*b*) buying in a manner designed to minimise stock levels.

The buyer

It is an anomaly of management structures generally that a good sales manager will invariably get to the very top while a successful buying manager rarely gets beyond middle management. Selling may carry the glamour status, but as regards a company's liquidity, the buyer has every bit as important an influence. He should have an inquiring mind, analytical ability, imagination and the necessary technical knowhow of his employer's trade.

The buying manager is one of the key appointments in a company and, like other such executives, he should be of the highest calibre the company can afford. If a company's gross profit margin is 25 per cent the salesmen will have to sell £400 of goods to equal the same result achieved by the buyer saving £100 of costs or expenses. This is what the trading account would show, but in liquidity terms the difference is even more marked since the avoidance of costs generally avoids altogether the investment of funds. Selling involves not only the funding of stocks and debtors, but the costs of administration, despatch, invoicing, sales ledger maintenance, debt collection etc.

It is a common saying that the best way to control money is before it is spent and, in practice, this necessitates a reliable ordering procedure. Many companies operate unnecessarily elaborate cheque-signing procedures in the belief that this is not only desirable from a security viewpoint, but effectively controls expenditure. The cheque-signing stage is, of course, too late to exercise control on liabilities being incurred. Control should be exercised by investing the authority to place orders solely with the buying department.

Buying, in this instance, should also include hiring for it has been known for executives to get around authorisation limits as regards capital purchases by just hiring the assets they want.

Order size

In times of liquidity difficulties, buyers should examine the economics of order size; smaller orders, even with a slightly higher unit price, will mean that less working capital is tied up. Some suppliers are glad to receive large 'commitment orders' and give their customers the option of taking small call-offs as they are required, but at prices based on large-order discounts.

The easiest way of avoiding a supplier's price increase is often to change to a cheaper material; this raises the technical subject of value analysis with which the buying manager should be conversant. He should also be continually reviewing his suppliers, searching for and evaluating alternative sources.

The buying department should be responsible for not only manufacturing and trade purchases, but for such consumables as stationery and costs like telephone charges. Stationery is a very common area of waste, with often many managers, and secretaries, taking upon themselves the authority to buy in small quantities items which take their fancy. Copying machines are a source of high profit to the suppliers on account of their misuse in customers' offices. An alert management, generally, will constantly look for cost savings.

Intergroup quotations

Buying from another company in the same group in competition with outside suppliers always calls for careful assessment. For example, a Buyer might be quoted:

Outside supplier	£80	Fellow subsidiary	£100

On those facts alone he would be tempted to place the order outside. However, on enquiring further, he might be given the following breakdown of the other Group company's price:

Direct costs		£50	Marginal costs
Overheads	— Variable	10	
	— Fixed	25	
Profit		15	
		£100	

Two points arise:

1 Considering the profit of £15 alone, this would be lost to the group were the outside supplier's quotation to be accepted. From the group's viewpoint, therefore, the quotation is really between £80 (outside) and £85 (inside)

2 £25 of the group-company price is, however, made up of overhead costs which would be incurred anyway. From the Group's viewpoint, therefore, the quotation is really between £80 (outside) and £60 (inside)

On purely economic grounds (delivery might be an important factor), only in the event of an outside supplier's quotation being less than the marginal costs of a fellow group company, should it be accepted.

Production has not been referred to under a separate subsection. This is not to suggest that its function is less important than, say, purchasing or selling, but the principal liquidity considerations which arise from the factory floor are (*a*) the optimum utilisation of resources and (*b*) the minimising of the investment in stock, particularly work-in-progress, which has been dealt with earlier in this chapter. (Capital investment in plant etc will be dealt with later.) Production planning, materials handling, wage structures and factory costing are among many manufacturing subjects which can affect profit (and thereby liquidity), but it is considered outside the scope of this book to make more than a passing reference to them.

Selling and pricing strategy

It was seen in Chapter 1, that finance was one of the more restraining influences on turnover — the capacity to finance the required extra working capital. It was suggested, too, in Chapter 2, that perhaps too many directors today are striving to increase sales 'at all costs' when (*a*) the company's results would be improved if the emphasis were on increasing margins and (*b*) its liquidity would be improved if the emphasis were on quality of sales. Many are the companies, today, whose profits as well as liquidity would be improved from a volume drop in turnover.

Reducing the product range

In a multi-product company or group, careful analysis is required of the different rates of contribution and the different levels of working-capital investment required by each product, with a view to allocating resources accordingly. Whole lines of products can often be dropped with advantage. Analysis may confirm the 80-20 rule: 20 per cent of the product range provides 80 per cent of the turnover. Conversely, the least popular 20 per cent of the product range may account for less than 5 per cent of the turnover — sales which the liquidity position would be more healthy without.

Eliminating small orders

The taking of small orders was referred to earlier from the accounting angle, there often being much benefit to be gained from raising quite substantially the minimum-order size. Analysis may confirm another version of the 80-20 rule: 20 per cent of customers account for 80 per cent of turnover. Again conversely, the 20 per cent of customers which provide the smallest orders may only account for 5 per cent of the turnover — sales which both the liquidity and profitability positions would be better without. A detailed analysis of past sales should be conducted to ascertain the likely effect on liquidity and profits (what level of administrative costs could be saved?) of losing 5, 10 or 15 per cent of sales represented by the smallest orders.

Other questions which managements can usefully pose (all with the ultimate objective of releasing more funds to be redeployed on perhaps larger and more profitable orders) are:

1 Is freight, packing, carriage and postage charged, if not on all deliveries, at least on those below a certain value?
2 When were the company's trading terms and conditions last reviewed? Does the company take deposits with orders? Does it require progress payments where there are custom-built products?
3 Are the sales division demanding unnecessarily high stocking and delivery services and credit terms?

These are the days when questions should abound and no 'old customs' should be regarded as beyond challenge.

Improving profit levels

Although 'liquidity-solving' may be the ulterior purpose, profit-making can make a significant contribution. There are three broad alternatives whereby profits can be improved:

1 By increasing the volume of sales
2 By reducing costs (manufacturing and administration)
3 By increasing selling prices

The first way requires an additional investment of funds and was considered in Chapter 4. The second category has been considered under a number of headings above; costs should, in any event, be kept under constant surveillance. The third method, instituting a price increase, is the one that acts the quickest both on the company's profitability (provided it does not significantly depress sales) and its liquidity. Pricing strategy is, therefore, one of the key considerations for management. Price/volume studies should be carried out on every line with immediate advantage being taken of opportunities to improve margins.

If the intention of the management is to increase the net trading profit of their company, expressed as a percentage of turnover, from say 15 per cent to 20 per cent, any one (or a combination) of the broad alternatives listed above could be adopted, and might be presented to them on the lines of Figure 6:1.

Figure 6:1 Examples of increased profitability from sales

	Existing Results	Method A	Method B	Method C	Method D
	£'000	£'000	£'000	£'000	£'000
Turnover	(100)	(114)	(100)	(105)	(104.6)
Marginal costs	67	76	63	67	67.0
Fixed overheads	18	18	17	18	17.6
Net profit before tax	(15)	(20)	(20)	(20)	(20.0)

Method (A) Raising sales by 14%
(B) Cutting *total* costs by 6%
(C) Raising prices by 5%
(D) Adjusting each alternative by 2¼%

Example of a funding restructure

To conclude Part 3, Figure 6:2 shows how a company's balance sheet can take two quite contrasting appearances depending upon the management's choice of course — either to let things drift until the size of the overdraft forces the bank to present an ultimatum, or to take advantage of the more permanent sources of finance which are available.

Figure 6:2 Illustration of funding choices

	Year 0 (before)	Year 2 Inaction	Year 2 Action	
	£'000	£'000	£'000	
Ordinary share capital	400	400	400	
Reserves	200	275	350	(*f*)
NET WORTH	600	675	750	
Mortgage loan	—	—	350	(*a*)
Deferred tax etc.	200	225	250	
CAPITAL EMPLOYED	800	900	1350	

	Year 0 (before) £'000	Year 2 Inaction £'000	Action £'000	
Property (at valuation)	500	500	500	
Plant and machinery etc.	450	650	650	
	950	1150	1150	
Hire-purchase	—	—	150	(*b*)
TANGIBLE FIXED ASSETS	950	1150	1000	
Trade investments	50	50	—	(*c*)
TOTAL FIXED ASSETS	1000	1200	1000	
Working capital	(200)	(300)	350	
TOTAL NET ASSETS	800	900	1350	
Stocks	400	750	650	(*d*)
Debtors	600	1000	1000	(*e*)
Cash at bank	—	—	300	
CURRENT ASSETS	1000	1750	1950	
Trade and Expense creditors Current tax and dividends	800	1200	800	(*g*)
Factor's advance	—	—	800	
Bank overdraft	400	850	—	
CURRENT LIABILITIES	1200	2050	1600	

The following points should be noted from the final column of Figure 6:2:

(*a*) A mortgage loan, for 20 years, has been arranged on the property. The loan equals 70 per cent of the valuation, and introduces the first element of gearing — in this case 47 per cent (£350,000: £750,000)

(*b*) The 'action company' has availed itself of the opportunity to buy some of its new plant on hire-purchase, which is tantamount in financial management to raising a five-year loan, thereby also introducing a further element of gearing, but, more importantly, a degree of permanence to its borrowings, finance which cannot suddenly be recalled

(*c*) The opportunity has been taken to dispose of a number of old trade investments, which no longer served any useful purpose
(*d*) Although as a result of changes of sales policy, the turnover of the 'action company' has been increased well above that of the 'inaction company' (a fact which is not evident itself from the balance sheets), by a progressive 'pruning' of unnecessary stocks the overall investment is now below that for the company with the lower volume of sales
(*e*) Although the sales of the 'action company' are higher, the total of debtors, through a more efficient credit control etc, are no greater. However, the opportunity has been taken to factor its debtors, thereby raising £800,000 of short-term debt. Two practical matters arise in this respect: (i) depending upon the exact legal ownership of the factored debts, some companies 'net off' the so-called 'advance' against total debtors, and (ii) in the instance illustrated, with a sizeable credit balance on its bank account, the company would probably take at least £300,000 less from its 'factor's advance' facility, using the full 80 per cent only when it had some use for such funds
(*f*) The higher reserves reflect the higher profits which have accrued from the whole rationalising programme carried out. It will be seen that the action company's capital employed (£1,350,000) now well exceeds that of the inaction company, a fact which, in itself, would call for greater profits if only to maintain the return
(*g*) The improved liquidity position has enabled the action company to stabilise its current creditor total, whereas the inaction company, with its overdraft already in excess of what the bank have agreed to, is almost daily in receipt of threatening letters and in serious risk of having all its supplies curtailed

Finally, it should be noted that the three columns of Figure 6:2 show ratios, respectively, as follows:

Current ratio	0.83	0.85	1.22*
Quick ratio	0.50	0.49	0.81*

*These figures will vary slightly depending upon how the factor's advance is shown in the accounts.

Part 4

Detailed planning

Part 4 deals with the various planning processes which should form a part of every company's management routine, preferably twice a year but at least annually, and which culminate in the adoption of the overall corporate plan and the detailed final budget for the ensuing period, usually 12 months.

Many managers in companies without a comprehensive system of budgetary control show little initiative for want of knowing how far they are permitted and expected to go in contributing to their company's achievements. That the overall success of a company depends very largely on the collective performance of its executives, both as planners and as managers, there can be little doubt. Their plans should be regarded as targets and, at the individual manager level, give the incumbents authority and objectives against which their individual performance can be measured.

Management in this context is not confined to directors and senior executives: foremen and corresponding administrative grades are part of a company's 'management' and, unless they are so treated and brought in to the corporate planning and the schemes for the development of shared objectives, the company will fail to obtain the best return it could from the salaries and other related costs it incurs.

For companies which either own a computer or have access to computer time, much of the donkey work of planning can be produced from such equipment ('off-the-peg' programs are available if required). Computers are particularly useful where it is necessary to establish either the 'best' result or, say, the least requirement for working capital from many alternative plans; the ability to assess rapidly, accurately and on an identical basis many variations of strategy, adds a new dimension to the decision-making processes of management. However, it is important that the information obtained from computers is interpreted by the appropriate experts and then set out in conventional form for management's deliberation. Thus the examples given later in Part 4 would be equally applicable whether the groundwork was carried out manually or on a computer.

Corporate plans, forecasts and budgets should clearly show what percentages have been allowed as the assumed increase due solely to inflation (not all items are likely to be identically affected). Sales forecasts should also show the increases and decreases in volume used as bases in each estimate.

7

Corporate planning and budgeting

When the skilled artist wishes to paint a picture, he does not approach the blank canvas in the first instance. There are various initial mental processes during which he determines the broad form of the picture's composition. Next, he may produce some rough outlines. Even when he has a clear idea of what he intends his final picture should look like, and stands before his canvas, he does not begin with the detail of one corner, he uses a broad brush and outlines the whole picture. Only when the balance is to his liking, will he begin in earnest to paint in the detail, firming up a bit at a time and not being afraid to change an emphasis here or a shading there.

The process of compiling budgets should follow a not dissimilar course and might, succinctly, be described as two phased: 'thinking big' and 'filling in the detail'. In particular, no operational budget should be developed very far without the corresponding cash and balance-sheet projections, first in outline and then in detail. These should all be developed in step with one another just as, for example, the production and sales divisions aim to produce a compatible plan.

A well known maxim states that no chain is stronger than its weakest link. It would be equally true to state that no budget can be more reliable than the accuracy of its component parts. If a sizeable expenditure budget has been wrongly calculated, or a sales forecast has been based on some wild guesstimating, the resulting cash projections will not, except by pure chance, provide an accurate guide for determining the financial requirements of the company.

Control before commitment

The general concept of 'control before commitment' is fundamental to a well run and financially sound company. Since it has been advocated that planning should be the basis for control, it follows that the controlling then becomes a process of making sure that the plans are fulfilled.

The very discipline of planning forces all levels of management to take a comprehensive look at the job they are being asked to become responsible for carrying out. This process, although it will not of itself solve any problems, should focus attention on the nature and extent of the difficulties which may be encountered. Such plans will also provide an advance indication of the financial requirements which will be needed to service the overall plan; this is particularly so in the case of further requirements for working capital.

The budgets will not be complete without balance-sheet projections, which will show the effect of the proposals on the financial structure of the company. These balance sheets provide an advance measurement of efficiency in financial terms before it is too late for corrective changes if these appear advisable. Such balance-sheet projections are, of course, also invaluable in putting up a case to a bank for extra borrowings etc.

The corporate plan

In too many companies the planning function is confined to (*a*) a one-year budgeting system plus (*b*) ad hoc special investigations. Medium-term and long-term planning is essential if a company is to develop along strategically and financially sound paths.

By definition, 'directors' are people entrusted with directing a company, pointing it in the right direction. If the board members concern themselves only with the managerial responsibilities in their respective divisions, they are failing in one of the most necessary collective duties of their office. This applies particularly to the director who is also the chief executive and who should devote at least one-third of his time to the future development of his company.

The broad strategic plan of the company or group, as a whole, is known as 'the corporate plan'. It should cover at a minimum three years ahead, with five years being the more normal and 10 years being more appropriate for companies with unusually long manufacturing cycles. (The numerical expression of the plan is considered in Chapter 9).

The corporate plan determines the broad framework and should be updated and agreed by the board of directors before the operational budgets are drafted for the year. It should focus attention on the basic objectives such as profitability, market share and geographical cover. The intermediate annual steps likely to be necessary if the ultimate target is to be attained should next be estimated, with the first of these providing the objective for the first twelve-monthly budgeting exercise.

The corporate plan should be reviewed, and revised as necessary, at least annually in the light of exterior influences (eg economic considerations and competitors' activities) and the results being achieved by the company against its own forecasts and plans.

What is forecasting?

A forecast is an assessment of a probable future happening. Even the street-corner evening newspaper seller needs to forecast his requirements based on his assessment of what he is capable of selling on each day of the week.

Forecasting should precede budgeting and calls for a careful look at what is likely to happen in terms of trends. Budgets, on the other hand, are based on the implications of the forecasts and relate to actual planned events.

Forecasting skill has an increasingly more important effect on industrial results in these days of rapid change. Indeed, a company which gets its market forecasts wrong can quickly find itself in serious financial trouble.

It should be clear, therefore, that there can be no worthwhile planning without forecasting. Alas, in many smaller companies there are attempts to forecast (the results) with little or no attempt to plan the approach route. If this all-important detailed planning operation is omitted, what may be called a budget will have no more value than the crystal-ball guesstimate.

The planning should centre around determining five objectives:

1 An attainable sales forecast
2 An attainable production target
3 A desirable profit result in relation to capital employed (this will have a first step when the gross profit margins are determined)
4 An economic level of capital expenditure
5 Operating within the limitations imposed by the funds available (their maximum utilisation whilst avoiding undue risk)

What is budgeting?

The fundamental purpose of a budget is to guide (through the expression of common objectives). A budget provides a yardstick against which actual progress can be measured and action initiated, when necessary, to bring the operation back on course. As a forward plan, it serves on the financial side as an invaluable indication of impending weaknesses and dangers.

As a planning exercise, production of the budget:

1 Enables the directors to decide, from the many alternatives they may study, which is the most practical and profitable policy to pursue
2 Provides a systematic approach involving all departments in apportioning responsibility for the overall objective

It concludes with the adoption of a series of interlocking budgets covering all the operational aspects of the company, thus ensuring that all the divisions are on the same course. If the budgets have been formulated by the cooperative action of all levels of management, they will invariably also generate a greater *esprit de corps* and a greater striving for accomplishment — both of which augur well for the company's future success.

Maintenance of predetermined standards
Budgets also serve as a means by which competitive and various predetermined standards can be maintained. For example, the management should clearly establish its policy on gross profit margins, numbers of days credit on debtors, stock turnover etc. Budgeting and, later, monitoring are the simplest and most effective means for ensuring that the company does achieve and maintain such standards, since failure to do so could put unprovided-for pressure on its liquidity.

Finally, it is essential that all levels of management should appreciate that a budget is not, of itself, an authority to spend money which should not be spent. Conversely, because an item of expenditure was not included in a budget is not, of itself, a reason for not seeking authority to incur the expense if it is clearly in the company's interest to do so.

Designing the budgetary control system

Space does not permit an exhaustive consideration of budgetary-control systems, but since the information given in or ascertainable from many companies' 'management accounts' represents so low a return in relation to the cost in salaries and other overheads of those engaged in collecting, processing and submitting the data, it is considered necessary to pass some constructive comments.

The management accounts should be the core of the internal information system, the data on which management judges, not only its performance, but what corrective actions may be necessary. And it is on these judgements and facts that the company's finances have to be planned and negotiated.

People who require information

The people who require information fall into three broad categories:

1 Those who guide the policy of the company — the directors
2 Those who control divisions of the company — the managers
3 Those who carry out day-to-day functions within the divisions — the buyers, the estimators, the foremen etc

The form of the management information circulated should aim to provide each of these levels with what they need in the most appropriate form. It will be obvious that such information should be supplied in different forms for the different operating levels.

Management's time is limited. Reports are often too bulky and fail to highlight the aspects where corrective action can be taken. Quality in reporting should be the aim, with a clear and logical layout of all figures — summarised results and trends for the policy makers, detailed breakdowns for the departmental managers. A good chief accountant should consider it his role not only to produce the information, but to assist the non-financially trained recipients in its interpretation and use (this is particularly so when a system is new or has been changed).

Management resistance

Stories are legion of management resistance to the introduction of a budgeting system in a company which has not previously involved lower levels of management in the planning procedures. The needs are for a most careful psychological approach if the company is to benefit from the very many hours which will be spent on fact-finding, debating and drawing up the so-called 'final budget'.

It is important that managers should be shown not only what is wanted of them, but what benefit they can obtain themselves from using the system in running their own departments. It is important, too, to distinguish in their minds the functions of:

1 Corporate planning — which is carried out in the highest management circles, with the results being passed down the line, and
2 Budgeting — which is carried out at all levels but builds up from the bottom. (The same course should be followed in the preparation of investment estimates)

All short-term budgets should be capable of achievement. They should not be based on 'ideals'.

Budgets should also always be drawn in line with the classifications of cost employed in the accounts department. If this is not done, the monthly comparison of 'actuals' with 'budgets' may become a formidable task.

Sales budget

A review of the sales prospects is usually the first step in the budgeting process. This is a most important forecast to get accurate since, very largely, all the cost and expenditure budgets are geared to it. But this is not to suggest that the sales division should be given rein to determine the policy of the company.

Sales forecasts should never be established simply on an arbitrary percentage uplift from the previous year, but rather built up from current considerations of market trends, the economic outlook, changes in product lines etc.

Alternative plans

It is not uncommon for the sales division to produce more than one plan. For example, estimates geared to either different levels of advertising or to choices of entering or not entering new territories. It will be for the budget officer to examine the expected costs, financial requirements and profits from each of these, leaving it to the board to evaluate the odds of success under each plan as compared with the expected profits.

For a sales forecast to be a reliable basis for budgeting, it is necessary for it to be broken down by the sales division into as many component parts as possible. For example:

1 Product lines (the profit margin may not be the same on each)
2 Markets, methods of sale, territories etc. (where these are likely to vary from the normal)
3 Month-by-month sales (for cash phasing purposes)
4 Trade discounts and any special terms likely to be agreed ('cash

discounts' do not affect selling and should be the responsibility of credit control)

Target value of orders
Finally, for the purposes of providing a yardstick for measuring activity in terms of actual selling achievement, it is necessary for the sales budget to be broken down into monthly 'orders to be taken' objectives — generally passed to the salesmen in the form of slightly inflated 'targets'. As is explained in Chapter 13, in all but some retail companies, the sales figures brought into the accounting are, of course, a direct reflection of the level of orders taken, often many months earlier. Very largely, therefore, the emphasis of control, and therefore on fixing realistic budgets, must be on this order-taking activity.

Budget committee

In large firms, corporate planning may be classified as a separate staff function. Budgeting is not some by-product of accounting, it is a management aid and, as such, it is better that it be placed in the corporate-planning area of responsibility rather than that of the accounts department. Accountants deal almost exclusively with facts in their day-to-day work and, unless they have had managerial experience elsewhere, tend not to be the best judges of likely future happenings, risks and uncertainties.

Budget officer
If there is no separate corporate-planning department, there should be a 'budget officer' who, at least in respect of his budgeting duties, should be responsible to the finance director. (If these duties do not occupy him fully, he could be the person charged with monitoring the liquidity position, producing graphs, weekly financial digests etc — dealt with in Part 5.)

In organisations of every size, the budget should be drawn up for submission to the board, by a committee comprised of representatives of selling, buying, manufacturing and finance. Either the budget officer or a representative of the corporate-planning department should also be a member of that committee.

A standard timetable for budgeting

What is a practical procedure in one company for producing the budgets, may not be in another. In most companies the procedure is begun too late with the result either that the following year's budget is not produced until well into that year, or that insufficient time is given to compiling and revising the figures.

The following is an attempt to show the main steps which should precede the submission of a budget for adoption by a board of directors, with a suggested timetable.

Four months before year-end

1 The budget committee collects all relevant facts and figures (past and future) together

2 The sales director reviews the sales potential with the budget committee in the light of all limiting factors:
   (*a*) external (eg market demand)
   (*b*) internal (eg production capacity)

3 The committee considers the tentative sales, production and profit targets in relation to the corporate plan

4 The committee produces the 'outline budgets', using broad assumptions, and circulates these to the senior levels of management for comment on the reasonableness of:
   (*a*) the broad assumptions adopted for their respective divisions, and
   (*b*) the various levels of operation suggested

5 The finance director arranges for the production of 'outline' cash-flow and balance-sheet forecasts, notes on essential ratios etc

Three months before year-end

6 The committee presents the board with the outline budget and obtains approval in principle. (The sales forecast should, at this point and in total, be considered by the sales director, as virtually his final budget objective)

7 The budget officer prepares and supplies each manager with:
   (*a*) a blank pro forma budget covering all his 'accountable costs' (see Chapter 11)
   (*b*) information on the current performance of his department; past budgets; trend figures and a list of the assumptions agreed upon by the board for planning purposes; and
   (*c*) information on corporate expectations for the new budget year

8 The purchasing officer may wish to place provisional material orders. Likewise, the personnel officer may wish to commence a recruiting programme

Two months before year-end

9 The managers draft their first rough detailed budgets; these they then attempt to sell to their 'line superiors'. (The budget officer attends such meetings to offer technical advice and to point out any inconsistencies with the corporate plan or other interdependent plans and budgets. These meetings should end with budgets to which the managers are personally committed to their line superiors)

10 The budget officer collates all the managers' budgets and presents them to the committee as a comparison with the outline budget (including liquidity and working-capital projections)

11 Meetings are held between the committee and those managers whose budgets, it is considered, should be revised

One month before year-end

12 The committee presents the board with the 'final budgets' for approval (including final cash-flow and balance-sheet projections, notes on essential ratios etc)

13 Subject to the board approving the 'final budgets', the budget officer issues every manager with details of his 'approved budget' (these now amount to his programme of activity for the year)

14 The managers prepare to put the budget plan into effect

Three to four months after year-end

15 The committee considers the desirability of revising the budgets for the second half-year. (This will generally arise from the budget no longer being capable of attainment in the light of external circumstances which did not exist when the first budget was drawn up)

Pricing the products

It is often found that sales prices are based on an approach no more scientific than adding a fixed percentage to the cost of production. This system overlooks market conditions which, as a general rule, invite profits to be higher when the demand is high; the profit level should then be reduced when the demand turns downwards. (All costs should be segregated into the usual fixed, semivariable and variable categories in order to determine the breakeven point of manufacture and the levels of extra sales needed to achieve given profit objectives.)

Price Code considerations apart, the 'right price' is, in effect, the highest the market will stand. In liquidity terms, as was suggested in the previous chapter, it is generally better for a company today to make its profits from a larger margin on a smaller turnover rather than vice versa.

Finance charges (external)

Two types of finance charges are found in management accounts. The first, which are also to be found in the company's financial accounts, are payments to outside parties (banks etc) for cash loans and other facilities (eg hire-purchase). The second are 'internal charges', made within groups and companies in order to make local managements more aware of the full cost of their investment decisions (see Chapter 11).

The external finance charges of a company should not be deducted from any set of accounts, management or financial, before the 'trading result' is struck. This is important, since two otherwise identical companies, one with all equity capital the other with high gearing, should show the same result to their executive managements. The board alone are responsible for determining the financial structure and, hence, the after-interest results.

In producing a company's budgets, it is not possible to calculate the external finance charges exactly until the month-by-month cash projections have been worked out, and the resulting level of overdraft or loans determined. For preliminary budgeting purposes, an approximate estimate is sufficient, but for final budget purposes, the interest figure should be accrued monthly as accurately as possible.

Contingency plans

Although the attainability of budgets can be claimed to be a direct function of the trouble taken in producing every figure, such best-laid plans have an unpleasant habit of not always working out too accurately in practice.

A failure to meet the sales forecast may not be very serious if production and the incurring of other directly related costs can be slowed down in time. A sizeable excess in sales, on the other hand, can generate production and finance problems.

Accordingly, budgets are often more useful, as both a guide and a control, if they are drawn up on a semiflexible basis. This can be as simple or as sophisticated as the circumstances dictate. In its simplest form, the variable overhead budgets would be geared (as the labour and material budgets usually are) by predetermined factors such as 'orders taken'. For example, if after a period these were more than a given percentage below expectations, this would trigger off certain economies aimed at bringing the profit back onto course by the year-end. Conversely, and also based on orders taken, predetermined favourable variances would permit, for example, extra despatch and invoice staff to be enrolled.

General and specific reserves
It is recommended that all budgets should incorporate:

1 A general contingency reserve — against completely unexpected happenings, and
2 Specific contingency reserves — against specified headings, where the extent of the expected cost cannot, at the time of drawing up the budget, be determined with any accuracy

An example of the function of a 'specific contingency reserve' frequently arises under the heading of 'labour' and concerns wage rates. A wage negotiation, scheduled for six months' time, is expected to put a rate up by between 10 and 20 per cent. On what basis should the budget be drawn up? It is advocated that the divisional budget should allow for no more than the 10 per cent increase (the minimum); additionally, a figure should be added to the 'specific contingency reserve' equal to the cost of that part of the settlement above 10 per cent, which the management considers it most likely it will have to settle for. (The recommended procedure for controlling these contingency reserves, which should not be created in respect of the less significant unknowns, is considered in Chapter 13.)

Two types of happening can cause fundamental variances to a company's overall budget:

1 Changed conditions externally (eg an unforeseen price increase in important raw materials or the collapse of a major customer)
2 The failure of a division to meet its objective (eg the breakdown of a key piece of machinery in the factory)

The causes will be either temporary or permanent in nature; if the latter, the entire budget should be revised, for it is, for all practical purposes, useless to operate on a budget which is no longer capable of achievement.

Budget changes after approval

A budget should not be thought of as sacrosanct, on the other hand if it is changed every time there is the least change in the assumptions upon which it was based, there is the risk (apart from the sheer cost and confusion to all levels of management) of the various departments working off different sets of figures.

Once the budget has been adopted by the board it should only be amended with their authority (see Chapter 13 for the suggested procedure). One practical exception to this may be acceptable, whereby a manager is enabled to reallocate certain of his budgeted overhead costs between expense headings.

'Two-way commitment'

The conclusion to the whole budget procedure should be a series of mutual commitments between, at the highest level, the divisional managers and the executive board; at various lower levels, between the managers and their respective divisional managers. Each manager commits himself to produce his budgeted result within the agreed level of cost; his superior commits himself to consider this level of expenditure as acceptable so long as the budgeted result, as evidenced by the monthly management accounts, is being achieved.

Return on capital employed

As was stated in Chapter 2, the maintenance of, or the improvement in, the return on capital employed will only be assured by featuring such considerations during the annual planning operation. These returns should be considered at the outline-budget stage, and no final budget should be approved without the relevant consequences being calculated.

In times of high inflation, requiring substantial increases in such directly unrewarding investments as working capital, it can prove very difficult for some companies to maintain their return on capital employed in the absence of running up a dangerously high trade-creditor position.

To achieve an improvement in the earnings per share, which shareholders normally expect to see each year, the board may have to consider, if the option is available, increasing long-term debt (on which interest charges are lower than on short-term loans), thereby improving profitability although increasing the capital-employed base and affecting adversely the return thereon.

8

Capital budgeting and project appraisal

Reference has already been made to the need to reappraise, from time to time, existing projects and all major investments (including property purchases and costly pieces of plant). Unless these reviews are carried out systematically, preferably on an annual basis just before beginning the next year's budgeting procedures, it is likely that uneconomical operations will be perpetuated.

Even if an operation is earning a 'just acceptable' return on the capital employed, it is worth considering its disposal if the funds so realised can be more profitably used elsewhere. In any such disposal assessment it is important to take account of any management and group overheads (eg a share of head-office costs) which are currently charged to that operation and which would still have to be met by the group after the disposal.

The return a large group can obtain from a particular operation (calculated after an allocation of group overheads) may be very much less than a smaller company or individual purchaser, without such overheads, could make from it — hence the price which can be negotiated often encourages the disposal of 'marginal' operations.

It should never be overlooked that an investment in new manufacturing assets, whether merely more modern units or a quite new project, invariably gives rise also to a need to increase the investment in working capital.

Capital budgeting

Apart from entirely new projects, dealt with below, investments in new fixed assets fall under two headings:

1 Replacement situations and
2 Improvement, expansion or reorganisation situations

Factory, transport and other managers who carry responsibility for fixed assets should be invited once a year to review their replacement requirements (about three months before each year-end) in the light of the outline budget denoting the ensuing level of operational activity anticipated. The company may have general policies on replacements (eg on cars — after 50,000 miles or three years, whichever is the earlier), but this should not discourage managers, particularly in the factory, from putting up early-replacement suggestions when these can be justified on economic grounds (eg output per hour, reduced manning or, simply, on technical grounds where changes can come quickly). Such proposals should be discussed initially with the buying department in order that their submission may be accompanied by up-to-date prices.

Economic evaluations

Companies may also have general policies about the desired annual level of new capital investment. But there can be dangers from too rigid an approach (eg in times of inflation, fewer items will be replaceable from a given allocation). A comprehensive evaluation of the economies which would attend each purchase should be the principal deciding factor — such evaluations including, of course, the opportunities available for funding, and the overall effect in the case of substantial purchases, on the gearing ratio, borrowing limits, etc.

There may be no clear demarcation between 'replacement' situations and what amounts to a new project. The evaluation report for both should be carried out by the corporate planning department or, in the smaller company, by the budget officer in conjunction with the divisional managers concerned.

Lead times

There can be considerable lead times on some larger pieces of equipment and if items of this kind are essential for the following year's operations it may be necessary for the board to authorise their purchase in advance of the final budget being approved. Indeed, it is not uncommon for some requests to be originated during the course of the year; this practice is to be discouraged since managers must be disciplined to think and to plan as far ahead as is necessary to avoid changes in the entirety of the budgeted plan on which the financial arrangements would all have been based.

New projects

It is, of course, impossible to arrange for all potential new projects to await the budget-producing period, in order that they can be assessed along with the company's other operations. By their nature, project opportunities tend to arise at unexpected times — and often from unexpected quarters. It is a short-sighted board which is so inflexible it refuses to consider a good idea for want of its being the correct administrative season.

Boards should encourage the submission of investment ideas, but should not attempt to allocate any specific sum for 'unknown projects' when finalising the annual budget. Several years may pass with no worthwhile submissions appearing; at other times, more than one may be under active consideration.

Merit classification

Where there are several projects (including the expansionary replacement of fixed assets), they should be classified, by mutual agreement of all the divisional managers affected, according to urgency and to merit, before submission to the board.

Many groups have diversified into products wholly alien to their own fields of activity. Some of these ventures have worked out satisfactorily, but many companies have come to regret their decisions, some as a result of not appreciating the management involvement which becomes necessary if the required background fund of knowledge is to be built up.

Cost of capital

A company considering the purchase of new capital equipment, a building or a whole new project, needs to judge it by criteria that are similar to those an independent investor should apply to any investment situation. It should require a minimum return for:

1 Giving up the use of the funds invested (even if these funds have to be borrowed, they represent funds which could be deployed elsewhere)
2 The business risk (ie of not getting either the cash back if the purpose of the investment fails, or the hoped-for results from it)
3 The loss in purchasing power (on account of inflation, the return on the shareholders' equity, though not on any 'non-indexed' borrowings, should compensate for the depreciating value of the

original outlay)

Right return for the risk
Currently, it is possible to earn about 10 per cent on short-term deposit-type investments, where the cash can, if required, be recovered within a matter of days. Many such deposits are, for all practical purposes, also 'riskless'. Short-term loans and overdrafts are costing companies between 11 and 15 per cent but for such funds to be utilised for, at best, unproven projects the company clearly should seek to earn a more than nominal surplus.

Some companies, in these uncertain days, are looking for as high a return as 25 to 30 per cent for new projects, and the average is probably about 20 per cent. (The rejection by companies of most projects with a decidely 'venture' element has served to bring this average rate down to a level which the sounder schemes can justify.) On simple replacements, with or without an expansionary element, a rate of little more than the cost of short-term funds may be acceptable provided the net profit on trading (ie before finance charges but after depreciation and an allocation of overheads) exceeds this cost.

Evaluation

The long-term success of a company hinges, very largely, on the correctness of the management's decisions on major capital expenditure. Evaluation involves calculating the long-term profitability after taking account of every quantifiable influence on the company, which means more than 'just doing the sums'. Depending upon the size of the project (each level of management should have authority to invest small sums in minor capital acquisitions), a very detailed investigation may be justified covering the operational and strategic, as well as the purely financial, aspects.

All capital outlay, however, should stem from the corporate plan and be a definite part of the company's long-term objectives. (Few decisions are more costly than a complete change of course necessitating the forced sale of relatively new capital purchases.)

Cost and risk
Every type of finance, whether its source is external or retained earnings, carries a cost and a risk. When used to acquire business assets, it must be ensured that the profits generated therefrom will be sufficient, in the long-term, to cover the costs and to compensate for the risks involved.

In large groups, financial analysts and economists are employed. In smaller companies capital-expenditure evaluations come within the finance director's personal sphere of operation. In practice, few managers have either the time or the skill to go to the lengths which the business-school academics advocate.

Discounted cash flow (DCF)

Net present value
Of the many alternative mathematical methods of evaluation, one stands out as the most practical (and simplest) for the average company director's use. This is the 'net present value' (NPV) method and includes, in one logical exercise, all cash considerations embracing:

1 Income and expenditure
2 Capital and revenue
3 Taxes, grants etc
4 The time value of money

NPV expresses all of these in terms of one common denominator — the net flow (either inflow or outflow) of cash.

In order to allow for the fourth consideration enumerated above, the time element, it is necessary to take account of the losses or gains arising as a direct result of paying or receiving cash at various dates. (No account of changes in purchasing power are meant in this respect.)

Lost opportunity cost
It is clear that to be paid £1000 today is worth more than if the £1000 were received in one, two or three years' time. During the interim years the opportunity would be lost to use the £1000 gainfully. This is called the 'lost opportunity cost' and is compensated for by discounting back to the present day all receipts (and payments) arising in the future.

Discounting, therefore, is the reverse of compounding. £1000 in 1, 2 or 3 years' time would, at 10 per cent a year compound interest, become £1100, £1210 and £1331 respectively. Conversely, therefore, cash inflows arising in 1, 2 and 3 years' time of £1100, £1210 and £1331 would each be said to have a present-day value of £1000.

In practice, if the rate of discount used in the calculation is the same as the rate of interest payable by the company on the borrowings it would have to raise (the 'cost of capital') then, broadly speaking, any overall inflow would represent profit. (Policies on writing off depreciation and grants, and creating tax-equalisation accounts can create differences compared with the figures taken into any one year of the financial accounts; the difference between credit sales and cash receipts from sales may also create a dissimilarity, particularly in the first trading year of a new project.)

Uses of DCF

DCF methods have the considerable advantage of providing accurate and consistent means for appraising and comparing capital investments. Their specific uses include assessing:

1 Whether an investment would provide a return greater than the cost of the funds invested in it
2 Which of a number of alternative investments would provide the greatest return
3 Whether the replacement of an existing asset would provide a greater return than maintaining the present, and less satisfactory, unit
4 Whether the abandonment of a partly completed project, if the circumstances have changed, would be more beneficial than its continuance

Practical examples of DCF

The following two examples of NPV methods of calculation, which for simplicity ignore the effects of inflation (considered later) should demonstrate its practical use and absence of mathematical complication. The DCF figures can be found from either discount tables or by using a simple pocket calculator (set up a 'constant division' of 1.075 once only for both examples, then divide each year's inflow or outflow in turn by the number of relevant years).

Proposed purchase of new plant

1 Corporation tax is taken at 50%
2 Capital cost in year 0: £100,000
3 Estimated scrap value in year 6: £5000
4 Grant (tax-free) receivable in year 1:£20,000
5 100 per cent first-year tax allowance receivable in year 2
6 Extra investment in working capital: £5000

7 Net cash revenue receipts in year 1: £20,000
year 2: £26,000
year 3: £24,000
year 4: £16,000
year 5: £14,000

8 Cost of capital: 15 per cent a year (7½ per cent after corporation tax)

9 It is assumed that, overall, the company is making taxable profits such that all tax allowances and tax-deductible charges are fully relieved

The calculation is set out in Figure 8:1, from which it will be seen that the project would barely cover its costs and would not appear, mathematically, as a very worthwhile investment. (The same example, but taking into account inflation, is shown in Figure 8:3.)

Figure 8:1 DCF calculation on an asset purchase

Years:	0	1	2	3	4	5	6
	£'000	£'000	£'000	£'000	£'000	£'000	£'000
Capital cost	-100						
Scale of scrap							+5
Grant		+20					
Tax relief			+50				-2*
Working capital		-5					+5
Net cash revenue receipts		+20	+26	+24	+16	+14	
Tax on revenue profits			-10	-13	-12	-8	-7
Cash inflow/outflow	-100	+35	+66	+11	+4	+6	+1
NPV (at 7½%)	-100	+33	+57	+9	+3	+4	+1
Net discounted cash inflow				+7			

*This figure represents the tax which would be paid in year 7 on the sale of scrap (discounted)

Comparision of alternatives

Cash flow in years 0 to 5 are as given in Figure 8:2. If the cost of capital is 15 per cent (7½ per cent after tax) and the company can raise only sufficient for two of the three projects it has under consideration, which should be discarded? It will be seen that NPV ranks project No. 2 as the 'best' and project No. 1 as marginally better than project No. 3.

Figure 8:2 DCF calculation on alternatives

	Project 1		Project 2		Project 3	
	Cash flow	DCF	Cash flow	DCF	Cash flow	DCF
	£'000	£'000	£'000	£'000	£'000	£'000
Year 0	-100	-100	-100	-100	-100	-100
Year 1	+40	+37.2	+50	+46.5	+10	+9.3
Year 2	+40	+34.6	+50	+43.3	+70	+60.6
Year 3	+40	+32.2	+40	+32.2	+60	+48.3
Year 4	+40	+30.0	+30	+22.5	+30	+22.5
Year 5	+40	+27.9	+30	+20.9	+30	+20.9
	+100		+100		+100	
NPV (at 7½%)		+61.9		+65.4		+61.6

DCF under inflationary conditions

It is an oversimplification to ignore inflation altogether in DCF calculations on the grounds that it affects all figures alike, but this is what the great majority of companies do; it is also what some business-school academics recommend.

First, the effects of inflation may be materially different on the items which constitute net cash revenue receipts. Sale prices may be under statutory control, labour and raw materials costs often do not move in identical cycles and overheads (eg rents) may have a sizeable fixed element.

Second, there are generally 'delay factors' between certain directly related items; for example, a cash outlay on capital equipment and the receipt of the relevant grant and tax relief. During times of significant rates of inflation, the value of such grants and tax relief is not the same as it appears to be when the investment is made. Conversely, since corporation tax on profits is paid 9 to 23 months after the year-end (15 to 29 months after the midpoint of the year), its cost in real terms is reduced. A 50 per cent tax rate effectively becomes about 35.5 per cent with inflation at 25 per cent a year if the tax is not paid until 12 months after the year-end.

Figure 8:3 DCF calculation with inflation

Years	0	1	2	3	4	5	6
Assumed rates of Inflation	—	25%	20%	15%	10%	10%	10%
Inflation factor	1.000	1.250	1.500	1.725	1.898	2.087	2.296
NPV discount factor	1.000	0.930	0.865	0.805	0.749	0.697	0.648
Inflation discount factor	1.000	0.800	0.667	0.580	0.527	0.479	0.436
'Composite' discount factor	1.000	0.744	0.577	0.467	0.395	0.334	0.283
	£'000	£'000	£'000	£'000	£'000	£'000	£'000
Capital cost	-100						
Sale of scrap							+11(6)
Grant		+20					
Tax relief			+50				- 5(7)
Working capital		- 6(1)	- 1	- 1	- 1	- 1	+10(6)
Net cash revenue receipts		+25(1)	+39(2)	+41(3)	+30(4)	+29(5)	
Tax on revenue profits			-12	-20	-21	-15	-15
Cash inflow/outflow	-100	+39	+76	+20	+8	+13	+1
NPV (at 7½%)	-100	+36	+66	+16	+6	+9	+1
Net discounted cash inflow				+34			
NPV (discounted by 'composite' factor)	-100	+29	+44	+9	+3	+4	0
Net discounted cash outflow				-11			

The number of years inflation which have been allowed for is shown in brackets after the figures affected

Inflation can have a not insignificant effect — enough to change what might appear as a marginally worthwhile project into one with negative appeal, or vice versa. The former is the case illustrated in Figure 8:3, which is based on the same facts as Figure 8:1 but takes into account the anticipated effects of inflation. In Figure 8:1 the project showed a net inflow, albeit a small one; after taking into account inflation, the result in financial terms reveals a net inflow of £34,000. However, when this is expressed in real terms, it becomes an outflow of £11,000, the main contributing factors being the delays in receiving both the grant and the tax relief.

9

Producing fund statements

What is a fund statement?

It is important to realise that the reference here is to 'funds' and not to cash alone; cash, as has been pointed out earlier, is just one of many forms of funds a company uses. But in whatever forms funds are received, at a point in time all obligations have to be met in cash, a fact which cash planning (see Chapter 10) must allow for. Indeed, the essence of successful liquidity management is the generation of sufficient cash as and when it is needed.

It is necessary to look at two balance sheets, one at the beginning of the period and the other at the end, in order to see how funds have flowed into a company and how they have been deployed. These movements are summarised on a 'fund statement', which consists of a pair of schedules, one showing the sources of any new funds, the other showing the form in which such funds have been used and are currently represented. Sometimes the two schedules are set out in one column in the form of a reconciliation.

Whichever method is chosen, the statement itself represents a reconciliation between two balance sheets and will itself always 'balance' since for every fund 'source' there is an 'application' (or 'use').

It should be noted that only the net movement of funds is shown on these statements. For example, inward movements of stock in a year might be £1,000,000 and outgoings £900,000. On the fund statement only the increase of £100,000 in the investment in stock would be shown.

Statutory requirements

Company financial accounts relating to accounting periods beginning on or after January 1976 must be accompanied by a 'statement of fund movements'. In anticipation of this, many companies have issued statements of 'sources and application of funds' during recent years. These have taken a number of forms, with many appearing as reconciliations of the overall movement in the cash and bank balances, as in Figure 9:1.

Figure 9:1 Statement of sources and application of funds

Source of funds		
Funds generated from operations:		
Profit for the year (before tax)	000	(*a*)
Taxation charged in accounts	(000)	(*a*)
Minority interest in net profits	(000)	(*b*)
Dividends charged in accounts	(000)	
RETAINED EARNINGS	000	
Provision for depreciation	000	
Credit from capital grants account	(000)	
Increase/(Decrease) in deferred taxation	000	
CASH FLOW	000	
Funds from other sources:		
Share capital	000	
Loan capital	000	
Capital grants received	000	
Hire-purchase finance	000	
Minority interests	000	(*b*)
	000	
Application of funds		
Purchases/(Sales) of fixed assets	000	
Increase/(Decrease) in working capital (excluding liquid funds)	000	(*c*)
	000	
MOVEMENT IN NET LIQUID FUNDS	000	

(*a*) The credit in respect of transfers from capital grants account is generally either credited direct to profit and loss account or offset against the tax charged against profits and is thus reflected in one of these two amounts
(*b*) Arises in group accounts only
(*c*) Individual movements in stock, debtors, creditors etc should be shown by way of note

Sources and uses

When considering the funds which a company will, or needs to, generate, it is convenient to view them as arising from the following sources:

1 Trading profits (before taxation)
2 Depreciation and amortisation (which have the effect of reducing the investment in fixed assets)
3 Increases in capital employed by way of:
 (*a*) new share capital
 (*b*) new loan capital
 (*c*) grants received
4 Decreases in net working capital by way of:
 (*a*) a decrease in stock
 (*b*) a decrease in debtors
 (*c*) a decrease in cash and bank balances
 (*d*) an increase in trade and expense creditors
 (*e*) an increase in bank overdraft
5 Decreases in fixed assets and investments (from disposals)

Similarly, the new funds arising can be considered as being utilised in the following ways:

1 Trading losses
2 The payment of dividends and taxation
3 Decreases in capital employed by way of:
 (*a*) redeemed share capital
 (*b*) repaid loan capital
4 Increases in net working capital by way of:
 (*a*) an increase in stock
 (*b*) an increase in debtors
 (*c*) an increase in cash and bank balances

(*d*) a decrease in trade and expense creditors
(*e*) a decrease in bank overdraft

5 Increases in fixed assets and investments from new purchases

Balance-sheet changes

Though the above summarises the categories of 'sources and uses' most commonly found, when quantifying forward plans and presenting them for critical examination, it is generally more convenient to follow actual balance-sheet changes. For example, reserves will change only by the amount of retained earnings (after taxation and dividends); thus the amount against the headings of dividends and taxation payable (including any setoff of grants) would be confined to the net changes and not the actual cash outgoings.

It is helpful to attach a summary of the effects of acquiring or disposing of subsidiary companies during the year, since otherwise the relevant amounts will become 'lost' in the overall group 'sources and uses' figures, thereby possibly clouding the significance of some important items.

Marshalling the relevant facts

It has been advocated that the corporate plan should cover a minimum of three years, with five years being the more normal and 10 years being the more appropriate for companies with unusually long manufacturing cycles.

It is also advocated that at least the first three years of this plan should be evaluated in terms of the funds it will require and the sources from which it is proposed those funds will be raised.

The many figures that it will be found necessary to amass before the plan finally emerges are normally compiled on separate schedules. Accuracy will be found to be not only a function of forecasting ability, but of the detail into which all levels of management are prepared to go in order to arrive at 'the best possible projections'.

One all-embracing statement

Many companies, having produced a number of individual divisional projections, fail to consolidate all the relevant facts into one all-embracing statement, and to show the proposed sources and uses of funds, for the benefit of their board, their bank manager and other parties affected. Only when the final process has been completed, and it is known that all the many schedules, forecasts and estimates really do interlock can it be claimed that the board have an agreed corporate plan.

The final summary, apart from the size of the figures on it, should take no materially different a form for a single small company than for an industrial group of 100 or more companies.

In Figures 9:2 and 9:3 are set out an example of the combined corporate plan and fund projection statement which it is strongly recommended every company should produce, at least once yearly, and adopt as its medium-term objective.

Producing a company's forward plans in this balance-sheet format affords the board an opportunity to consider the financial position as shareholders and others will probably see it from published accounts in the years ahead. If the public view is considered likely to be unfavourable, it should not be too late for the board to take an alternative course in order to eliminate the weaknesses.

Taxation liabilities

The value of all cash projections can be seriously undermined if incorrect allowance is made for the due payment of taxation. The annual corporation-tax liability for a profitable company can be the largest single outlay of the year and, unless this is adequately provided for, can severely disrupt the otherwise carefully planned financial resources.

Care, too, must be taken not to overlook such obscure liabilities as advance corporation tax, which becomes payable shortly after a dividend is paid. Few companies deal with their own tax affairs, employing instead either their auditors or a special tax adviser. It is strongly recommended that, just prior to starting the annual budget procedures advocated, the tax advisers be asked to state the liabilities the company will face during (*a*) the year ahead — accurate figures should be available — and (*b*) the following year — a fairly accurate estimate should be possible, but it may be necessary for the company to indicate its expected level of profits, dividends payable and capital investment in the current year.

A practical format

It will be seen that the layout for fund statements advocated in this book, which is not concerned with requirements for published accounts, begins on the left with the most recent known facts — the most recent audited balance sheet. This affords an indisputable base from which the projections will, naturally, become less certain the further into the future they are extended.

Figure 9:2 Projected trading results (3 years)

	Estimated Current Year	Projected		
		Year 1	Year 2	Year 3
Trading, profit and loss account	£'000	£'000	£'000	£'000
Sales	(3500)	(4500)	(6000)	(8750)
Cost of sales	2200	2825	4000	5750
GROSS PROFIT	(1300)	(1675)	(2000)	(3000)
Selling costs and other overheads	800	1010	1280	1780
Depreciation	80	90	110	250
TRADING PROFIT	(420)	(575)	(610)	(970)
Interest charges	70	85	150	200
Non-trading items	—	—	—	—
NET PROFIT BEFORE TAX	(350)	(490)	(460)	(770)
Taxation (less grants)	100	160	100	200
Dividends	50	55	60	70
RETAINED EARNINGS	(200)	(275)	(300)	(500)
Volume sales increase		5%	10%	25%
General inflation rate assumed		25%	20%	15%
Cash flow	280	365	410	750
Capital employed (average)	2030	2343	2985	3770
Working capital (average)	505	707	930	1270
Stock (average)	550	700	975	1325
Debtors (average)*	900	1150	1575	2075
Trade and expense creditors (average)*	600	675	900	1225
Stock ratio (No. months)	3.0	3.0	2.9	2.8
Debtors ratio (No. months)	2.9	2.8	2.9	2.6
Creditors ratio (No. months)	2.2	1.9	1.8	1.8
Profit ratio (gross profit %)	37.1	37.2	33.3	34.3
Trading profit (% of sales)	12.0	12.8	10.2	11.1
Net profit (% of sales)	10.0	10.9	7.7	8.8

Sales : working capital	6.9	6.4	6.5	6.9
Trading profit : working capital	0.8	0.8	0.7	0.8
Interest cover	6.0	6.8	4.1	4.9
Return on capital employed (%)	20.7	24.5	20.4	25.7
Earnings per ordinary share**	47.6p	63.6p	69.6p	111.6p

* 2/27th of each figure represents VAT (at 8 per cent) which is disregarded in calculating the debtors ratios and creditors ratios
** 500,000 £1 ordinary shares — 'Earnings' equal after-tax profits less dividends payable to preference shareholders.

In Chapter 7 a suggested timetable was given for the production of the annual budgets and for updating the corporate plan. This procedure would normally begin about four months before the year-end at a time when:

1 The previous year's accounts would probably have been audited and adopted at the annual general meeting, and
2 The management accounts for the first six or seven months of the current year would be to hand

From these particulars it should not be difficult to estimate reasonably accurately:

1 The current year's results
2 The current year's sources and uses of funds, and
3 The balance sheet at the end of the current year

Armed with these facts, the requirement is to assess the immediate future in terms of likely trading achievement and fund requirements with each projected year-end balance sheet effectively 'proving' the intermediate figures. Ratios, calculated as in Figure 9:2 will be found most helpful, but it must be emphasized that a plan which is based only on 'percentage uplifts' will be discovered to be ill-founded and of no great practical use (by all means note, for example, the expected overall volume change in sales, but let that figure emerge from the detailed makeup and not be the basis of the whole sales plan).

Ratios, as in the example shown, should as far as balance-sheet figures are concerned (eg capital employed and working capital) be based upon average figures obtained from the projected opening and closing balance sheets for each year.

Figure 9:3 Projected fund statement (3 years)

	Actual latest audited balance sheet	Estimated: Current year fund		En ye bal sh
		Sources	Uses	
Balance sheet	£'000	£'000	£'000	£'
Ordinary share capital	500			
Reserves	500	200		
Adjustments (re value)	50			
EQUITY INTEREST	1050			1
Preference shares (6%)	200			
NET WORTH	1250			1
Mortgage debenture				
Debenture stock	200			
Deferred tax, grants, etc	450	60		
CAPITAL EMPLOYED	1900			2
Property	890			
Machinery etc. (w.d.v.)	600		70	
Hire-purchase				
TOTAL FIXED ASSETS	1490			1
Net current assets	410		190	
TOTAL NET ASSETS	1900	260	260	2
Working capital				
Stocks	500		100	
Debtors	800		200	1
Factor's advance				
Cash at bank				
CURRENT ASSETS	1300			1
Trade and expense creditors	600			
Current taxation	75	5		
Dividends payable	25	5		
Bank overdraft	190	100		
CURRENT LIABILITIES	890		190	1
Current ratio	1.46			1
Quick ratio	0.90			1
Gearing (%)	19.0			16

Year 1 Fund		End of year 1 balance sheet	Year 2 Fund		End of year 2 balance sheet	Year 3 Fund		End of year 3 balance sheet
ces	Uses		Sources	Uses		Sources	Uses	
0	£'000	£'000	£'000	£'000	£'000	£'000	£'000	£'000
		500			500			500
5		975	300		1275	500		1775
		50	50		100			100
		1525			1875			2375
		200			200			200
		1725			2075			2575
			400		400			400
		200			200			200
0		600	170		770	150		920
		2525			3445			4095
		890		410	1300		100	1400
	150	820		780	1600		400	2000
			500		(500)	300		(800)
		1710			2400			2600
	215	815		230	1045		450	1495
5	365	2525	1420	1420	3445	950	950	4095
	200	800		350	1150		350	1500
	300	1300		550	1850		450	2300
			700		(700)	100		(800)
							45	45
		2100			2300			3045
0		750	300		1050	350		1400
0		100	60		160		60	100
5		35	5		40	10		50
0		400		395	5		5	
	215	1285		230	1255		450	1550
		1.63			1.83			1.96
		1.01			0.92			1.00
		13.1			32.0			25.3

Comments on example

The illustration is an example of what a company can achieve without a liquidity problem even if it is faced, over a period of three years, with a forecast 72.5 per cent cumulative rate of inflation and a planned 150 per cent expansion in sales.

In the period of these three years, the company expects to extend its factory at a cost of £510,000 and to invest £1,780,000 in buying new plant and machinery. It achieves this and emerges with a stronger balance sheet (from a small earnings retention equal to slightly less than 6 per cent of turnover). It is planning a small reduction in its margins and its trading profits, expressed as a percentage of turnover, are also lower; accordingly, it does not expect trouble on account of price controls.

It proposes raising a mortgage debenture of £400,000 and, at the end, expects to have £800,000 outstanding on hire-purchase and a further £800,000 advanced by its factors; it expects its overdraft to have been repaid and the period of credit it takes from its suppliers should have been slightly reduced in line with the modest improvement it expects on its own debtor and stock positions.

Earnings per share

Above all, the earnings per ordinary share are planned to rise from 47.6p to 111.6p — a rise of 134 per cent which the shareholders should find most satisfactory, being almost twice the expected increase in the rate of inflation over the same period.

These are the plans which, if 'everything' goes according to plan should emerge as the actual results. But what if 'things' do not go according to plan? The capital purchases should all be delayed to the last practical moment and be reassessed at the first sign of sales beginning to fall short of budget. The hire-purchase and factoring commitments should largely be capable of self-adjustment in any such changed circumstances. The factory building and mortgage loan may well be an early commitment, but the interest cover should be adequate to ride any reasonable deferment in the company's expansion plans.

Calculating the stock requirement

As has already been intimated, Figures 9:2 and 9:3 are overall summaries of many supporting schedules. One of these will provide the basis for the stock figures; in respect of the amount at the end of year 1 (£800,000), this might be arrived at as shown in Figure 9:4.

It has been estimated:

1 Factory production will, as is normal for this company, take six weeks
2 Raw materials (bought in bulk) will, on average, be held for four weeks before being consumed
3 Finished goods will be held in stock for an average of five weeks. However, during the final quarter of the year (on which the year-end stock levels are based) production is to be permitted to run ahead of sales requirements in order to meet a seasonal 'peak' in sales the following quarter, hence there will be an expected further £90,000 of finished goods by the end of the 13th week. (Note: It is not being assumed that the production level will be above average; if this were the case, an adjustment would be necessary to work-in-progress as well)

Figure 9:4 Computation of stock levels

Budget for fourth quarter of year 1

	£'000	£'000
Sales		1300
Manufacturing costs:		
Materials	275	
Direct labour	385	
Factory overheads	250	
	910	
Increase in physical stock levels	(90)	
Cost of sales		820
Gross trading profit		480

(The effects of inflation have been allowed for in the above figures)

Stock (£'000)	
Raw materials (4/13) x 275	84.6
Work-in-progress	
Materials: (6/13) x 275	126.9
Labour: ½ x (6/13) x 385	88.8
Overheads: ½ x (6/13) x 250	57.7
Finished goods:	
(5/13) x 910 + 90	440.0
	798.0

Similar calculations would be made for debtors and for creditors, remembering to allow for VAT.

10

Producing cash-flow projections

In the context of this chapter, 'cash flow' means a company's day-to-day cash receipts and payments.

It is important to bear two facts in mind when producing cash-flow projections:

1 Sales do not equal 'cash in the bank'. It is necessary to be realistic on collection forecasts
2 It is generally considered easiest to forecast expenditure accurately, sales next and cash least easily

It is most important, therefore, that a reasonable margin be allowed in producing these projections, particularly if the company is running at the limit of its overdraft facility.

In essence, the production of a cash-flow projection (necessary in order to identify the timing and magnitude of the cash needs) consists of estimating in cash terms, and generally in 12 one-monthly steps, the various transactions which have been projected in total for year 1 of the corporate plan. The importance was stressed earlier of building up the company's future plans and budgets in outline initially to ensure their overall feasibility. The cash projections must feature in the preliminary exercise since, if the company cannot finance its 'peak' cash requirement, it becomes necessary to start the thinking and planning afresh.

The cashier's viewpoint

It can be said that a statement of sources and uses of funds expresses the financial manager's viewpoint; a cash-flow statement, on the other hand, expresses the cashier's viewpoint of the same set of transactions. It is, in fact, possible to obtain a complete summary of the cash receipts and payments from examining together (*a*) a fund statement and (*b*) the same period's profit and loss account. Figure 10:1 shows the relevant figures for year 1 of the example given in Figures 9:2 and 9:3 (for simplicity, VAT has been ignored).

Figure 10:1 Comparison between financial manager's and cashier's views of the same transactions

	Financial manager £'000			Cashier £'000	
Liquidity position (opening overdraft)	(290)			(290)	
Cash flow (retained profit + depreciation)	365	(*a*)			
Increase in working capital (excluding cash)	(325)	(*b*)	Payments	(4310)	(*d*)
Capital expenditure	(240)	(*c*)	Receipts	4200	(*e*)
Increase in deferred tax, grants etc.	90				
Liquidity position (closing overdraft)	(400)			(400)	

NOTES (£'000):

(*a*) 90 + 275 = 365

(*b*) 215 + (400 − 290) = 325

(*c*) 820 + 90 − 670 = 240

(*d*)	600 + (2825 + 200 + 1010 + 85) − 750 =	3970
	(80 + 510) + 160 − (100 + 600) =	50
	30 + 55 − 35 =	50
	820 + 90 − 670 =	240
		4310

(*e*) 1000 + 45000 − 1300 = 4200

The timespans to plan

It is recommended that, as a minimum, companies should produce cash-flow projections for year 1 of the corporate plan consisting of monthly figures for the first three months and quarterly thereafter (with monthly figures being produced quarterly in advance as the year progresses). If the company has a seasonal trade, the year-1 projections should be computed monthly for the whole year (with updatings as necessary).

The fund statement should provide a reliable guide to the cash requirements at the end of years 2 and 3; however, if the company either has a seasonal trade or there are periods when it seems there may be an extra strain on the available cash resources (eg when its main corporation-tax liability has to be met), quarterly projections should be made for years 2 and 3 as well.

Short-term plans, generally on a weekly basis, are considered under the management aspects of liquidity in Part 5.

Marshalling the relevant facts

Obviously, the starting point for monthly cash planning is the forecast opening balance sheet, with the intermediate steps reconciling to the projected year-end balance sheet. This concept of planning the route from balance sheet to balance sheet is considered important in liquidity management; in practice, it is found useful to produce the intermediate balance sheets (see Figure 10:3) both by way of 'proving' the cash-flow arithmetic and as a basis for monthly balance-sheet monitoring (see Part 5).

It has already been stressed that no plan can, except by pure chance, achieve a greater degree of accuracy than the data upon which it was based. Virtually all cash transactions are a reflection of income or expenditure, but this is not to suggest that, when expressing these in cash terms, it is not possible to introduce further degrees of inaccuracy. The 'phasing' of the receipts and payments can have a marked effect on the level of a company's bank account.

Accordingly, it is necessary to allocate adequate time to this phasing process which, for convenience, will be considered under four headings:

1 *Cash receipts from sales*

Each month's forecast sales should be phased into expected months of cash receipts based on (*a*) past experience and (*b*) any changed circumstances (eg cash discount changes, special contractual terms and the general economic situation). An example of a phasing schedule is given in Figure 10:2.

Figure 10:2 Phased cash receipts from sales

	Month 1 £'000	Month 2 £'000	Month 3 £'000	Month 4 £'000	Month 5 £'000	Month 6 £'000	. . .	Total for year £'000
Sales*	300	310	320	350	375	400		
VAT**	24	25	26	28	30	32		
	324	335	346	378	405	432		
Collections:								
2 months (15%)			48.6	50.3	51.9	56.7		
3 months (70%)				226.8	234.5	242.2		
4 months (15%)					48.6	50.3		
			48.6	277.1	335.0	349.2		
Total debtors at beginning of year (£1,000,000)	275.0	300.0	276.4	73.6	50.0	25.0		
	275.0	300.0	325.0	350.7	385.0	374.2		

* Assuming no cash sales
** Export and other sales not subject to VAT should be appropriately separated

2 *Cash payments to suppliers and expenses*
Each month's forecast purchases and expenses should be phased (on a similar schedule to Figure 10:2) into expected months of cash payments based, as for sales, on past experience and the consideration of individual items (eg rates would be payable half-yearly; a percentage of salaries and wages, representing PAYE, would be payable monthly in arrears).

Purchases and expenses may conveniently be summarised under (*a*) items which bear no VAT (*b*) items which bear the normal VAT rate and (*c*) items which bear different rates.

3 *Cash payments on capital investments*
Phasing schedules should be prepared, taking into account any deposits which may be payable and any grants the company expects to receive. If it is proposed to finance any acquisitions by way of hire-purchase, it is convenient to include the expected amounts receivable and instalments repayable.

4 *All other cash payments and receipts*
Phasing expectations for all other planned transactions should be considered and scheduled. This should include not only corporation tax, which has already been referred to, but provision for either receiving or paying the quarterly net amounts of VAT.

A practical format

The importance of reconciling the cash-flow projections with the relevant opening and closing balance sheets on the corporate plan has already been referred to. It is also important that all the many schedules and supporting schedules which generally have to be prepared should be summarised on one all-embracing statement — a cash-flow plan which can be readily understood by those of the management who have not been financially trained. Figure 10:3 is an example of the type of cash-flow statement it is advocated should, together with the updated corporate plan and coming year's budgets, be placed before the board of directors. (Up-dated versions of the cash-flow projection should be prepared and submitted quarterly.)

Figure 10:3 Projected cash-flow statement (1 year)

	Estimated end-of-year balance sheet £'000	Cash month 1 £'000	Bala she a end mo £'00
BALANCE SHEET			
Ordinary share capital	500		50
Reserves	700		72
Adjustments (re value)	50		5
EQUITY INTEREST	1250		127
Preference shares	200		20
NET WORTH	1450		147
Debenture stock	200		20
Deferred tax, grants etc.	510		53
CAPITAL EMPLOYED	2160		221
Property	890		89
Machinery etc (w.d.v.)	670	50	71
TOTAL FIXED ASSETS	1560		160
Net current assets	600		60
TOTAL NET ASSETS	2160		221
WORKING CAPITAL			
Stock	600		62
Debtors	1000	(275)	104
CURRENT ASSETS	1600		167
Trade and expense creditors	575	260	66
VAT account	25		[illegible]
Current taxation	80		[illegible]
Dividends payable	30		[illegible]
Bank overdraft	290	(35)(*e*)	32
CURRENT LIABILITIES	1000		10

*Figures for months 4 to 12 have been omitted

sh nth 2 00	Balance sheet at end of month 2 £'000	Cash month 3 £'000	Balance sheet at end of month 3 £'000	*	Balance sheet at end of month 12 £'000
	500		500		500
	750(a)		775(*a*)		975
	50		50		50
	1300		1325		1525
	200		200		200
	1500		1525		1725
	200		200		200
	560		485		600
	2260		2210		2525
	890		890		890
	704(*b*)	100	796(*b*)		820
	1594		1686		1710
	666		524		815
	2260		2210		2525
	650		650		800
))	1084 (*c*)	(325)	1105 (*c*)		1300
	1734		1755		2100
4	650(*d*)	245	689(*d*)		720
5	4		8		30
	80	80	100 (*f*)		100
	30	30			35
(*e*)	304	(130)(*e*)	434		400
	1068		1231		1285

Notes on Figure 10:3

(*a*) For monthly budget purposes, it is sufficient to adopt an appropriate flat tax rate, in this example 50 per cent, with perhaps a more accurate calculation taking place in the final month. (The accrual of the following year's tax liability does not affect the current year's cash position)

(*b*) Depreciation has been assumed at £8000 per month

(*c*) A summary of how the monthly debtors projections are arrived at is as follows:

	Month 1	Month 2	Month 3
	£'000	£'000	£'000
Opening balance	1000	1049	1084
Sales for month	300	310	320
VAT thereon	24	25	26
Cash received	(275)	(300)	(325)
Closing balance	1049	1084	1105

(*d*) A summary of how the monthly trade creditors projections are arrived at is as follows:

	Month 1	Month 2	Month 3
	£'000	£'000	£'000
Opening balance	575	604	650
Cost of sales / Overheads	242	252	262
Stock increase	25	25	—
VAT thereon	22	23	22
Cash payments	(260)	(254)	(245)
Closing balance	604	650	689

(*e*) These figures represent the net monthly inflow or outflow of cash expected. Arithmetically, they should 'cast' vertically and horizontally

(*f*) This £100,000 represents the tax which at this point of time becomes payable within 12 months — hence its transfer from deferred tax to current liabilities

Constraint of an overdraft limit

Many companies, as a direct result of inflation, are finding their plans restricted by the amount that they are able to borrow. With many of the usual sources for term finance either closed or being ultra-selective, it is to the local bank manager that companies are being forced to turn in more than usual proportions. But in times of economic uncertainty the clearing banks, also, have become more selective, and more cautious generally.

A company which has produced its tentative corporate plan and fund statements will know approximately the facility it is going to require. If, as is now common, such plans reveal a need to increase the bank facilities quite considerably, it is prudent to seek an immediate conference with the bank. The outcome of this may well be that the company is offered some increase, but not to the extent necessary to achieve the whole of its outline plans.

Plan in reverse

In such instances, the revised planning is carried out, more or less, in reverse. The maximum monthly facilities offered (with a margin for contingencies) are inserted in the cash-flow projections, and the various manufacturing and sales plans modified appropriately. (It being assumed, of course, that the company has exhausted all its opportunities for releasing 'inert funds' etc. in accordance with the advice given in Part 3 of this book.)

It is not sufficient just to apply a fixed pro rata change to all the estimates. Business does not work like that, since there are costs which vary directly or partially with turnover, and others which are unaffected. All costs should be appropriately classified and, from such an exercise, it is generally possible to produce a number of interrelated formulae. From these it then becomes a question of determining the optimum level of operation which can be undertaken within the cash facility available, and seeing whether this is likely to yield a worthwhile profit.

Part 5

Practical management

It is not possible to draw a clear demarcation between liquidity management and other aspects of financial management; the two are interrelated and, very largely, interdependent. Similarly, there is no obvious divide between financial management and general management; both turn on the effective organisation and control of resources and have many common objectives. Accordingly, parts of the final chapters in this book may appear to fall outside the scope of pure financial management. References to general management have been limited, as far as possible, to the salient and relevant points, but readers with wider experience will know that it is difficult, if not impossible, to maintain an efficient financial discipline in the centre of a basically disorganised corporate environment.

The final part of this book deals with the practical management operation, the effectiveness of which very largely hinges on the ability of all levels of management to work, not only individually to individual budgets, but collectively towards achieving corporate objectives. In turn, the ability so to work lies, very largely, in the hands of the executive board who must first create the right organisational structure, the subject of the next chapter.

Psychology is a major contributer to successful man-management, and its importance in financial management should not be underrated. For example, if a manager sees that the operational budget for his department is someone else's work, he will have little vested interest in seeing its targets are achieved. His pride will not be at stake. Who produces each budget is possibly as important as the budget itself. It follows, therefore, that the person who will be held responsible for its achievement should be the one who produces it for his superior's approval. (Never should other departments' budgets be fixed by the accounts department or the budget officer.)

11

Establishing lines of responsibility

For all levels of management to work in concord and with the greatest possible effect, the administration must be first class; above all, the lines of communication must be clearly defined, must be generally known and must be seen to work.

Organisation structure

Business management consists of getting things done through people and will be briefly considered under 5 headings:

1 *Organisation*
An organisation chart should exist and its contents be accessible to all levels of staff. Every individual should know clearly to whom he is accountable and for what; he should, likewise, know for whom he is accountable and the parameters of each such person's activities.

2 *Delegation*
The concept of accountability should never imply a bar to the delegation of parts of that responsibility, provided the delegator realises he remains accountable for the overall result. Good managers recognise that one of the main tasks of management is to lead and not to stifle initiative. They are executives who both surround themselves with the best subordinates they can find and are not frightened to delegate to those able to benefit therefrom, both the company and themselves. Poor managers are those who lack confidence and show it by employing weak subordinates and keeping everything close to their chests.

The strength of a company can often be more readily discerned at the middle-management level than around the boardroom table, and weakly managed divisions often have an adverse effect well outside their own immediate areas of responsibility.

3 Direction

Clear lines of communication, from the chief executive to the labourer on the workbench, should not only be defined, but they should be used. This is not to suggest a general prohibition of constructive discussion between persons with no direct communicating 'line' on the organisation tree, but rather that no orders should be given or taken without at least both parties' common superior concurring. If this simple rule is frequently broken, muddles proliferate, blame is disowned and friction soon grows.

Lower levels of management are not mind-readers and are dependent upon their immediate superiors for information about what is supposed to be happening and what precise role is expected of each man. Therefore, down the appropriate lines of communication clear and unequivocal instructions should flow and, whenever possible, these should be committed to writing.

But instructions are not sufficient. Good administration, it is advocated, consists of perhaps 10 per cent giving instructions and 90 per cent in seeing that those given the instructions both carry them out and carry them out properly.

It was seen earlier that as far as is practical, budgets should be produced by the persons who are going to be responsible for their achievement. It follows, therefore, that, as a basic concept, operating decisions should be taken at the lowest possible levels consistent with efficiency.

4 Coordination

One important function of all levels of management is to reconcile the conflicting interests of persons one or more levels down the organisation tree. This is largely a question of ensuring that practical and unambiguous instructions are given at the correct level — ie above the potentially conflicting areas. It is for the superior level of management giving the instruction to make it clear what each subordinate has to do; it is not for the two or more junior managers to 'work it out between themselves'.

5 Resolution

Undoubtedly, the respect that subordinates have for their superiors has a direct bearing on their work effectiveness. To a large extent, this respect is earned by the degree of decisiveness exercised. Business calls for a procession of decision-making and someone who is prone to vacillate or is forever countermanding his instructions can be a liability. If such a person manages to secure a position of authority in a company, the repercussions can be serious both in terms of financial results and in management development generally. Additionally, such persons are often 'buck-passers' or, because they have little self-confidence, are for ever seeking the confirmation of higher levels of management on simple decisions, which are well within their own sphere of authority.

Incidence of financial responsibility

If the company or group is not already so divided, it should be structured into 'operating divisions', each with a man at the head who is responsible for its profitability in line with the previously approved budgets.

The divisions should then be structured into departments, which are usually termed either 'profit centres' (where there is an element of either external or internal income or earnings) or 'cost centres'. Again, each should have a man at the head; one man may be responsible for more than one centre.

All incidences of responsibility, whether for financial results or otherwise, must be made obvious. If this is not so, it becomes all too easy for managers to blame one another, or the company in general, when things go wrong.

A manager should only be held responsible for results when:

1 It has been communicated to him:
 (*a*) what results he is currently achieving (ie the progress he is making towards his or his department's agreed objectives), and
 (*b*) what results he is expected to achieve in the future, and
2 It is within his power, if not completely to regulate what is happening, at least to have a major influence on the outcome

On the financial side, the processes of producing the budgets will focus attention on the staff organisation and should help to ensure that:

1 Individual responsibilities are clearly defined, and
2 The requisite authority, commensurable with that responsibility, is delegated

In larger groups, it is common for the parent board to determine the corporate strategy and then to leave the subsidiary companies' boards to run their companies more or less autonomously.

Responsibility for liquidity

The management structure should show in whom the ultimate responsibility for the company's or group's liquidity rests. There may be a group financial director and a group treasurer, with financial directors and financial controllers in each subsidiary. But however much latitude in financial management is delegated 'down the line', in every company or group, there must be one person with overall responsibility to the top board for liquidity management. That person must know the responsibility with which he is charged and all other levels of management must be left in no doubt that he is the man who is going to exercise the requisite authority over the whole company or group.

Accountability

The concept of accountability has two facets. First, it requires that each item of financial cost or income should be made the responsibility of a named individual; this should include even such apparently uncontrollable costs as rates (which, incidently, with the right degree of dynamism, can often be made to yield some ground). Second, every accounting statement, report etc should show clearly who is responsible for each result or group of results reported upon.

Thus the management accounts should distinguish for each section within a department, for each department within a company and for each company within a group, what are the 'accountable results' and what are the 'allocations' of uncontrollable costs (eg an allocation of head-office overheads).

Accountable results

It is generally convenient to design the relevant account or report sheets with the 'accountable' items scheduled first, coming down to a subtotal termed the 'accountable result'. (see Figure 12:1) This result may show a profit if the sheet refers to a profit centre, say, the sales division or a section thereof; it would show a 'loss' (ie a total cost) if the sheet referred to was a 'cost centre', say, the typing pool.

It can have a salutary effect on the results if the name of the individual responsible for each accountable result appears at the top of the relevant sheet or sheets. It can be surprising, too, how a manager's attitude towards his own position in a company changes when he is left in no doubt that his colleagues are aware of the extent of *his* financial responsibility.

Allocations

It is important that each manager, whatever his level, be given the 'allocations' relevant to his department. First, this enables the overall result of a department to be readily available and, second, it is often possible, as a result of a manager jibbing at the high costs allocated to his department or division (although he is not responsible for them) for useful suggestions for savings to emerge.

It follows that a company's budgets must build up, from departments through divisions and companies, to the group results on precisely the same pattern as the layout on the organisation tree. Thereafter, the responsibility for actual performance can be attributed to specific individuals or groups.

It may be useful for certain divisions and departments to have the relevant parts of their results re-summarised in order to show variable and semivariable costs in relation to turnover, output etc, and for these supplementary sheets to be circulated with the basic form of the management accounts.

Finance charges (internal)

One of the best ways in which to make managers conscious of the 'cost of capital' involved in the assets utilised in their departments or divisions is to raise appropriate charges against those units for the use of company or group funds.

To be effective, such internal charging does not have to be too sophisticated; indeed, a lot of the benefit will be countered if the administration aspects become too involved. It is sufficient, for example, with regard to fixed assets to calculate the interest charge on (*a*) the written-down value at the beginning of the year and (*b*) the cost (less grants) of any acquisitions during the year.

Such interest charges should, of course, feature in the planning stages of the budget and should result in managers assessing that much more carefully, the necessity for their operating units having new pieces of expensive plant and machinery.

The rate of interest chosen, it is suggested, should be at least as high as the rate paid on any current short-term company borrowings. This rate will then produce more meaningful 'after-interest' profit results from the individual divisions, helping to establish those which can or cannot justify their levels of capital investment.

Group holding company
In groups of companies, the parent company is very often a non-trading holding company; it is convenient for it also to operate as banker for the group. The parent will thus arrange all borrowings, it will be responsible for investing all surpluses and will lend such funds as may be required to its subsidiary companies.

It is essential that all senior executives in a group should be aware of their ability to influence, not only the level of capital investment, but also the level of working capital in their companies. Accordingly, if charges are made for all loans to the subsidiary companies, the chief executive in each will have a direct incentive to minimise his stock levels and to collect his debts with the minimum of delay. It is advocated, therefore, that the day-to-day control of cash and working capital be decentralised, and vested in the operating managers, meanwhile reserving to the parent company the overall responsibility for both arranging the sources of group funds and their strict monitoring in accordance with the corporate plan.

Under such an arrangement, it is generally more convenient for the parent company itself to own all group properties, which are then available for offering as security for group borrowings (the properties are rented to the subsidiaries on commercial terms).

Marshalling group resources

Every group of companies should have a definite policy with regard to the disposition of profits generated in the subsidiary companies; these profits should not be regarded by the respective managing directors as being automatically available in their own company for future investment purposes. First, if the parent is of the non-trading type, it will almost certainly have insufficient income to satisfy the payment of its dividends and will require to receive commensurable sums from the subsidiaries. Second, the group board is charged with producing the best results possible from the group as a whole; it may well be that the profits made in one subsidiary could make more for the group if, the following year, they were deployed in another quarter altogether. It is for the various subsidiary-company managing directors to make out their respective 'cases', but it is for the parent board alone to pronounce judgement.

Passing up profits

It is strongly recommended, therefore, that it should be group policy for subsidiaries with no outside shareholders to pass up (by way of dividend or as management charges or whatever method is preferred) at least annually to their parent, all available profits. This policy, which should naturally be built into the budgets, enables the group board, as part of a generally recognised discipline:

1 To control the use of all capital employed within the whole group
2 To require subsidiary-company managing directors to justify every part of their borrowing requirements (and not just in respect of capital purchases)
3 If there is an overall insufficiency of funds available, to rank these in the order judged to produce the best group result (generally, in terms of the expected surplus profits in each subsidiary after allowing the internal interest charge on its requested intercompany borrowings)

Such is the current pressure on many group financial resources, that the control of working capital is being singled out for special budget consideration with divisions being required to operate within strictly defined limits.

Intercompany profits

In Chapter 6 attention was drawn to the importance of buying managers being properly informed about the makeup of another group-company's prices when it is competing with a third party for an order. Some groups have a policy of not permitting their subsidiaries to make 'intercompany' profits, but such prohibitions are not recommended for several reasons:

1 It is against the general policy, advocated in this book, of making all managers not only 'profit accountable', but in competition with one another for group resources (based, very largely, on their respective trading successes)
2 It draws attention to occasions when group quotations are above those of competitors. The causes should always be investigated; if it is

found that no basic fault lies with the fellow subsidiary, it is suggested (in line with the recommendation in Chapter 6) that the group company's quotation be accepted and that the buying subsidiary be passed a credit from the parent for the cost it would otherwise incur by being forced to purchase above an 'open market price'. It is important that the friendly rivalry of managers should not be spoilt by the feeling of unfair transactions being imposed upon them

3 It will produce unnecessary variances if the output estimated for (*a*) outside customers' and (*b*) 'group customers' has to be differently priced

Intercompany profits have to be eliminated in the published financial accounts, and it is recommended that an appropriate reserve should be estimated and deducted in the summary of results in each set of monthly management accounts produced. (If this is not done, it is all too easy for an overoptimistic profit figure to become established in the minds of directors.)

Role of the outside specialist

Reference has already been made to the role of the 'City financial adviser', with his entrées to sources for funds, and to the tax adviser; also to the professional auditor (Chapter 2) and the mistaken belief which many small companies operate under, namely that their auditor is in some way partly responsible for managing the company's finances.

An outside specialist, sometimes called a 'company doctor', is often called in when it has become apparent to an executive board that their company is in dire straits and it is probably beyond their capacity to save it.

Comparatively few companies, however, seek specialist financial advice between these extremes. This is surprising since, for example, in the field of liquidity management the specialist can usually not only justify his fee relatively quickly, but can often divert a company from any as yet unnoticed cash crisis which is building up. If remedial action is not taken when the danger is relatively small, it may result ultimately in the need for action on a devastating scale.

The 'liquidity specialist' should be able to quantify the company's needs relatively quickly in the light of an in-depth study of its management accounts and budgets, and will then advise the board generally on the best steps to take regarding both (*a*) any impending trouble and (*b*) the managing of the company's liquidity in the future in order to avert recurrent crises. The outside specialist will have the added advantage in some boardrooms that he is likely to be listened to more intently than a colleague who is seen every day. And when the specialist speaks of overtrading or the like, it will be a very foolish board which does not heed the warning.

Periodic independent financial assessment

There are, undoubtedly, few companies or groups today which would not benefit — some very materially — from a periodic independent financial assessment of their businesses. This further very worthwhile role of the outside liquidity specialist falls under two headings:

1 To give a critical appraisal of the company's past trading achievements (say for three years) and its ability in liquidity terms to face the future, and
2 To provide the board of directors with a sounding board for its plans and aspirations, again with special reference to the constraints of its liquidity position.

Part-time liquidity management

For the smaller company, whose size does not justify the employment of a full-time treasurer, liquidity management can often be provided as economically by an outside specialist on a regular part-time basis, as by charging an existing senior executive with the specific responsibility to the board.

There is, also, the role of the outside specialist as a 'temporary' either to help supervise or actually to produce much of the figure work during the 'budget season', when the production of a large quantity of extra financial planning work undoubtedly places considerable strain on the staff of most small and medium-sized companies. Normal staff complements generally carry a day-to-day load that is sufficient to occupy normal hours. If the whole extra budget operation is left to be carried out during overtime hours (for which few managers are generally paid extra), it is unlikely that the best results will be obtained.

Internal audit

Most companies of modest size have an internal audit department. At one end of the scale, this can be as small as one man, whose role has no greater objective than to try to save on audit fees (ie the annual charge of the external auditor) by carrying out various routine checks with the emphasis on accuracy (eg the correct classification of expense items). In the large industrial groups, the internal audit department enjoys a high status in recognition of its many responsibilities.

There are three broad areas of activity for internal audit departments:

1 Checking an accuracy. As already indicated, the main function here is to check the accuracy of both the financial and management records, accounts, reports and estimates. Procedures are periodically tested, the allocations of expenses vouched and controls generally appraised
2 Deterring misfeasances. The emphasis in this case is on the prevention of any misappropriations of company funds
3 Appraising investment decisions. The role here, a common one in North American corporations, is to test management decisions before they are put into practice and to provide continuing processes of re-evaluation with a view to determining the best economic course of action in the light of changing external conditions

Line responsibility
Under the third category, the internal auditor would generally work alongside the corporate planning department and be responsible to the chief executive. The first two categories are often found in line responsibility to the chief accountant which, in reality, is wrong. If the incumbents are to be of maximum value to the company, they should owe no direct loyalities to the manager or staff whose work they will be primarily checking. In general, it is practical for the department to be directly responsible to either the financial director or financial controller.

Management by objectives

In recent years, there has been a slight shift in some companies away from budgets as the sole means of monitoring the attainment of objectives. The system of 'management by objectives' (MBO) has evolved.

The main characteristics of MBO, as compared with budgets (which, by their nature, seek to control all the components in one budget alike) is that MBO focuses attention on a few carefully chosen 'key factors' in the corporate plan and, for lower levels of the staff, in their respective divisional and departmental budgets. Easily identifiable objectives for individual members of the staff (or groups of the labour force) are agreed with the persons concerned; there is a reviewing process subsequently, with the establishment of slightly more ambitious objectives, and so on.

MBO has been known to improve productivity not only in manufacturing divisions, but also in the administration areas. But the system should only be regarded as an adjunct to, and never a replacement for, budgeting, which remains the most effective overall controlling discipline.

New legislation

No businessman of the United Kingdom needs reminding that, particularly in recent years, governments have legislated for and against corporate entities 'by the ton'. In most companies it falls to the company secretary to be the watchdog for such new Acts as may affect his company. But his interests will centre around those statutes with which the company has to comply. He may well not be alerted to watch out for changes in the benefits to which companies become entitled such as new types of grants and alterations in tax reliefs (which might, for example, make leasing more advantageous than hire-purchase or vice versa).

It is necessary for there to be a clear understanding between the company secretary and the finance manager on who is responsible for keeping himself fully informed about all financial changes which might affect the company, whether they originate as Acts of Parliament, from local authorities or any other source.

12

Disseminating Management information

Management and financial accounts

Past accounts have only a limited value to management, and even in the smallest companies it is necessary to understand the very different purposes for which historical and management accounts are produced.

Financial Accounts
These are mandatory (once each year) and are prepared on a historical basis (their relevance is likely to be particularly out of date in times of high inflation). They are produced for shareholders (as a report on how their directors have handled their investment), for creditors and would-be creditors (as a report on the financial standing of the company) and the tax inspector (for the purpose of assessment). The aim is that the figures should be as near 'dead accurate' as possible and, to this end, the figures are very often not finalised for three, six or even 12 months after the year-end. The accuracy of the figures has to be reported upon by independent auditors.

Management Accounts
These are confidential financial reports on the current state of the company. They are produced for various levels of management to enable them to measure progress and to be an up-to-date source of information upon which to take policy decisions. The aim is that the figures should be circulated quickly and to this end degrees of approximation are acceptable. Independent auditors are not involved.

The 'accountable result'

It follows from the previous chapter that 'allocations' to a particular manager's sheet must be made up of the 'accountable costs' of some other manager or managers. Such 'allocations' should be both logical and complete and, in order that these requirements may be known generally by the more senior levels of management, it is suggested that both the inwards and outwards allocations be shown. The broad principle is set out in Figure 12:1 ('profit centres' would not normally have allocations outwards).

Figure 12:1 'Accountable' layout for management accounts

. . . cost centre	**Accountable manager: Mr . . .**
Accountable items:	£'000
...	XXX
...	XXX
...	XXX
Accountable result	XXX
Allocations inwards:	
Head-office overheads	XXX
Accommodation costs	XXX
...	XXX
...	XXX
Total costs	XXX
Allocations outwards:	
Sales division	(XXX)
Factory division	(XXX)
...	(XXX)
...	(XXX)

Disseminating copies of accounts
Each divisional manager should be given:

1 Separate accounts for each of his departments — showing the accountable result for each subordinate manager, and
2 An account for the division as a whole — showing his own accountable result

The board of directors should be given:

1 Copies of the divisional acounts (it is usually unnecessary to provide copies of individual departmental results above the divisional level unless a report of a particular department has been called for) and
2 An account for the company as a whole. If the company is part of a group, the parent board may only require, depending upon the circumstances, to see the summarised results of companies for which the chief executives are accountable

It will be seen that if the principle advocated above (and illustrated in Figure 12:1), namely the allocation of all 'total result' costs, is carried to its logical conclusion then the company's final profit will be the sum of the accountable results of just the profit centres. For control purposes, however, it is strongly recommended that the overall company results be summarised both ways for presentation to its executive management, namely:

1 Schedule of the accountable results of the various divisions, which in total equal the company result, and
2 Schedule of the final results of all profit centres, which in total also equal the company result (as in (1)), but give a clearer idea of which profit centres contributed the most after taking into account all logically chargeable costs

Allocating costs

Allocations to other departments or divisions should not be on a wholly arbitrary basis, though there is a limit to the value a company would obtain from instituting too parsimonious an approach to the internal charging of general costs. Accommodation costs, for example, can be made on a floor-area basis with rates, light and heat being allocated pro rata in the absence of a logical reason to the contrary.

The detailed allocation of factory overheads is a subject outside the compass of this book, but small manufacturing firms, where sophisticated systems may not be warranted, should be careful to ensure that:

1 Their estimating (for quotation purposes) does take account of a reasonable allocation of overheads, prepared on a logical basis. For example, it would be prima facie wrong to allocate the same amount of costs to each machine if some occupied materially more space than others, or used more workers or more power, and

2 The oncost included in the pricing (to recover these overheads) is based as logically as possible on material costs, labour or a combination of the two or on machine-hours and is related to a level of turnover which is conservatively regarded as being attainable. Any under-recovery is of the nature of an unrecoverable loss as can be seen from Figure 12:2.

Figure 12:2 Under-or over- recovery of overheads

	Estimated result £'000	Actual 10% less £'000	Actual 10% more £'000
Transfer 'sales'*	(1000)	(900)	(1100)
Direct costs (50%)	500	450	550
Fixed overheads: £200,000			
Overhead oncost at 40% of direct costs	200	180	220
Profit on sales	(300)	(270)	(330)
Under-/(over-) recovery of overheads	—	20	(20)
Factory profit	(300)	(250)	(350)

*It is common for a manufacturing division to 'sell' its output to the sales division of the same company (for onward sale to the public) at a profit

Practical considerations

It is worth considering briefly a few practical points about the information a company should have available for its management:

1 Returns and accounts should be designed to match the recipients' levels of intelligence (remember, too, that many directors are not 'figure men')
2 All information which is recorded and circulated should aim to be useful, and not merely of interest
3 At all times the value of the information should be weighed against the cost of getting it out. Questions should be posed such as: Does it

matter? Can we improve profitability by knowing this or that for the future?

4 Executive control can only be effectively exercised if objectives are established, and reported upon, in detail rather than in aggregate. For example, sales should be controlled by (*a*) products, (*b*) areas, (*c*) salesmen etc as well as being looked at *in toto*

Contents and recipients

The distribution of management information should be reviewed regularly under two headings:

1 Contents. Such questions should be posed as: Are the contents still appropriate? Can the information be made more useful? Can it be made more intelligible? Is this, or similar information, already assembled in some corner privately(information which should be either superseded or more widely circulated)? If some departments are keeping their own records it is a sure pointer to the fact that they find it unsatisfactory to get such information quickly from a central source

2 Recipients. Can every recipient on the circulation list actually *do* anything as a result of being supplied with the information? Senders of regularly issued returns are entitled to assume the recipients all require such information unless they are told to the contrary (changes of systems and staff often lead to copies no longer being necessary, and there is often psychological resistance by managers to requesting the deletion of their own names). But returns should not be arbitrarily cut out without the recipients' concurrence, since such action provides a wonderful excuse for 'adverse variances' later on.

Issue information quickly

As a broad principle, the lower the level of management the sooner the information should be in the manager's hands. Also, the longer the delay in producing information, the less value it usually is for control purposes. Thus, as a general rule, data should be issued no later than the following:

1 Daily figures — by the end of the following day
2 Weekly figures — by the second day of the following week
3 Monthly (or 4/5-weekly) figures — by the end of the second week of the following period

The following are a few of the most common reports issued:

1 Daily:
  (*a*)Orders received
  (*b*)Orders delivered
  (*c*)Excess costs
2 Weekly:
  (*a*)Orders-received summary
  (*b*)Orders-delivered summary
  (*c*)Orders-in-hand summary
  (*d*)Excess-costs summary
  (*e*)Factory-output summaries
  (*f*)Materials costs and variances
  (*g*)Labour costs, overtime worked and variances
  (*h*)Expense summary and variances

(The above are 'activity reports' and are not directly related to the liquidity position, the recommendations on which are considered later.)

Review meetings

The management accounts and other reports should always be circulated in advance of the review meetings to enable managers:

1 To be appraised of their results before they are called upon to justify them, and
2 To obtain such explanations as they require for variances etc

The success of the budgets, as both a planning and coordinating technique, should be periodically evaluated in addition to the normal adjudication of individual managers' results.

Comparative figures

It was seen earlier (Chapter 7) that if planning is to be the basis for control, it follows that the controlling becomes a process of making sure that the plans are fulfilled. The effectiveness of the most carefully laid plans may, therefore, be to little avail if the subsequent comparison operation is omitted.

Budgets are not generally broken down into timespans of less than single calendar months, or the equivalent number of weeks, for the monitoring and reporting processes. Accordingly, the first obvious comparison to set out for each heading of income and expenditure is 'actual for month' against 'budget for month'. (Cost-accounting reports will, of course, deal in much greater detail with the *causa* of the overall profit variance (and variances from 'standards'), explaining this item by item and differentiating between the variances arising from changes in output level and from changes in actual material and other factory costs.)

Cumulative figures

The month's figures will reveal the variances which have arisen, but in isolation these give little idea of how the company is trading generally (any month can be exceptional). The usual practice is to give 'year-to-date' figures as well, but here the emphasis is wholly on the company's financial year, which may have little relevance to the trading cycle or, indeed, the timespan of the corporate plan. If a company's financial year does not coincide with its marketing year, and for taxation or other reasons it is not advisable to alter the financial year-end, there is much to be said for the management accounts showing the cumulative effect of one year's corporate plan (if this practice is adopted, it is necessary that the whole budget process be timed to coincide).

However, many companies prefer to have no clear annual aspect to their management reporting in the belief that business is a continuing process and, whether it is seasonal or not, is virtually unaffected by arbitary cutoff dates. Many of these companies choose to prepare 'moving annual total' (MAT) figures (which also lend themselves conveniently to the use of simple 'trend graphs'). These figures show the most recent 12 months (or 52 weeks) — generally in total, but are sometimes averaged down to a monthly level so that they have a greater affinity with the current month's figures. (Wisely, there can be but few companies left which still present their data on a 'this year as compared with last year' basis, which is virtually useless for management purposes.)

Clarity of presentation

It is advocated that the management accounts format outlined in Figure 12:2 would, in practice, consist of four columns of figures:

1 Budget for the month (or 4-4-5-week period)
2 'Actual' for the same period

3 Cumulative budget for either the most recent 12 reporting periods or for the 'marketing year' to date (the latter is recommended as being more relevant to current trading conditions and objectives)
4 Cumulative 'actual' on the same basis as (3)

(The 'actual' figures for one month should never include corrections in respect of a previous period. Only the cumulative figures should be amended, with an appropriate footnote if the adjustment is significant.)

It is important neither to give management too much detail nor to spoil the clarity of the accounts by including too many figures on a single sheet. Notwithstanding this, it can be very pertinent, and therefore useful, to place a column of percentages besides those figures where the relationship with certain others, for example income and costs, is of particular relevance to the final results.

Reporting periods

Should the so-called 'monthly figures' (budget and 'actuals') cover actual calendar months (ie be of varying numbers of days), 13 four-week periods or 12 '4-4-5-week' periods?

There are some businesses, mostly retail, where it is convenient and not illogical to work on calendar months. The planning unit for manufacturing, however, is almost always determined in weeks (if not in days), with the calendar month being virtually an irrelevance. With few exceptions for bank holidays, the week is a consistent unit of operating time and should be so adopted for control purposes. There is, however, one very compelling reason for choosing to base the monthly accounts and reports on a '4-4-5' cycle.

The cash cycle

However the company chooses to organise its internal affairs, it will have little control over its trading with both suppliers and customers. In the great majority of cases, trading companies work on a calendar-monthly cycle of statements and settlements. Accordingly, since liquidity management is one of the most important aspects, it is logical to produce the periodic liquidity reports, balance sheets and other such 'controls' on as near a calendar-monthly basis as is practical. If the '13 x 4' weekly basis is chosen, for more than half the year the management accounts will not coincide, to the extent of more than seven days, with the calendar month-end, the best suited time for reviewing the liquidity position. The '4-4-5' weekly basis (with a '4-5-5' about every fifth year) can be so arranged that this never ends more than four days either side of the calendar month-end.

13

Monitoring the financial results

Managing is basically a forward-looking process of taking current decisions with the future in mind. To function efficiently financially, the management must be in possession of the most up-to-date information from:

1 External sources — eg published statistics and economic forecasts
2 Internal sources — accounts, reports, trend statistics etc

From the relevant internally produced management data, the financial manager, be he a director, controller or whoever, will (*a*) be informed of the current position and (*b*) be required to take any appropriate action aimed either (if the basic circumstances have not changed) at bringing the company's finances back onto the course planned, or (if the basic circumstances have changed — eg sales have exceeded expectations) at steering the company's finances onto an equally sure course in the changed conditions.

Monitoring programme

Monitoring, it is claimed, is every bit as important as planning and, like the budget-forming processes, will vary from company to company. But much will be common to all businesses and the following checklists should provide a general indication of the main 'tabs' the financial manager should keep on his company's progress, with particular emphasis on the liquidity aspects.

There should exist in every company a definite monitoring programme; if this is not drawn up and adhered to, liquidity ratios and the like may only be calculated or studied when it is suddenly feared that the position has deteriorated. By this time, when actual fears have been engendered, it will almost certainly be unnecessarily late for corrective action; in other words, such action will need to be more intense than would otherwise have been the case.

The efficient monitoring of ratios should alert the financial management at the first signs of any change in the underlying financial stability of the company.

Virtually every company's monitoring programme should legislate for the following areas of control:

1 Orders in hand (the pending sales)
2 The immediate availability of cash
3 The six 'essential ratios'

Each of these will be described in greater detail later.

Orders in hand

It is necessary in both planning and monitoring to guard against too great an emphasis on sales figures at the expense of 'orders taken' and 'orders in hand'. 'Sales', in the accounting sense, refers to completed sales, transactions which have been delivered and invoiced; transactions from which, in the trading sense, the company has no further expectations.

A company's future sales are, except for any retail counter trade, wholly dependent on the orders its salesmen take weeks, months and occasionally even years before the actual sale features as such to the benefit of the company. Indeed, a declining company can often continue producing 'sales' well after its orders have dried up.

Unplanned changes in activity

Accordingly, the forward-looking processes of financial management must be alert to any variations in the order level which may herald an unplanned change in activity. Manufacturing companies are largely geared to the level of their 'orders in hand', the balance between orders taken and deliveries and a more than temporary drop in the level of planned orders in hand must initiate examination of the advisability of slowing down production.

Some companies find it useful to calculate various 'order ratios', which seek to quantify, generally in numbers of days, the volume of production activity represented by the orders in hand.

Daily programme

Each day, the financial manager should arrange to have compiled, as a minimum, the following data for review within his department. He should then study this objectively and alert any managers who should be made aware of any apparent departure from what has been planned.

1 Orders received (usually compiled by the sales division) and deliveries effected
2 Cash position as shown by:
   (*a*) the cash book and
   (*b*) the statement received from the bank
3 Updated forecast of the end-of-week cash position with notes on the reason for any changes

Weekly programme

The weekly procedure should divide itself on the financial side into: (*a*) a review of the past week's performance and the end-of-week position, and (*b*) compiling a definite cash plan for the ensuing week which, as far as the bank position permits, should conform with the objectives of the month's cash projection.

The following data should be obtained or compiled and then reviewed:

1 Orders received, deliveries effected (this should be at least numerically reconciled with the invoices issued) and level of orders-in-hand. These 'actuals' should be compared with the month's or 4/5 weeks' budgets. (It may be convenient to plot some of these figures graphically — possibly as, say, three-monthly running totals so as to eliminate weekly variations)
2 Factory data regarding output, material costs and variances, labour costs, overtime worked and variances, stock levels etc. Output should be compared with the 4/5 weekly objectives in the budget and the level of sales being achieved. (Bonus and overtime data will be required by the wages department as soon as available and will affect the wages liability in the weekly cash plan.)
3 Cash collections should be reviewed with the month's expectations. An overdue-accounts schedule should be scrutinised with the credit

controller, and an estimate made of the following week's expected cash collections

4 Schedules of payments for the coming week should be compiled, dividing the items into:
   (*a*) Liabilities which it is essential be discharged — including, of course, wages
   (*b*) Settlements which have been definitely promised
   (*c*) Payments that are desirable — for example, in order to obtain a cash discount
   (*d*) Payments which should be made in the current month but not necessarily in a particular week

   It is essential to allow a reasonable margin in scheduling payments on account of the unpredictability of cash receipts

Monthly programme

The monthly procedure consists of:

1 Reviewing the past 4/5 weeks' results and the end-of-month position
2 Compiling a definite cash plan for the ensuing month in the light of the end-of-month position relative to the forecast balance sheet at this time
3 Preparing and circulating the month's management accounts together with the financial manager's report thereon

For inclusion with the monthly accounts, the financial manager should compile with the aid of the operating managers, an up-to-date estimate of either the current financial year's or the current corporate plan's results. To achieve this, some companies get their managers to prepare each month an estimate for their respective divisions or departments of the year-end variances. The financial manager then produces a statement for the directors on the lines illustrated in Figure 13:1.

Data to be compiled
The following data should be obtained or compiled monthly and then reviewed:

1 Orders position (as for weeks)
2 Factory output, variance reports etc (as for weeks)
3 Summarised cash collections and payments for the past month — for comparison with the cash projections drawn up as part of the budget

procedure

4 An up-to-date projection of cash receipts and payments for the ensuing month, which should also be compared with the original cash projection
5 Calculate the 'essential ratios' (plus other ratios appropriate to the particular trade or company) — see below

(Note: Companies without efficient stock records — in value as well as in volume — may need to calculate their theoretical stock value each month on a 'cost of sales' formula, with accurate stock-takes being undertaken every, say, third or sixth month.)

Figure 13:1 Year-end results estimate

	Budget £'000	'Actual' £'000
Month 7		
Profit for year-to-date per management accounts	(750)	(820)
Months 8 to 12		
Budgeted profit	(450)	(450)
Expected adverse variances		75
Months 1 to 12		
Contingency budgets	100	
Authorised to date		30
Expected further calls		80
FINAL RESULT NOW FORECAST	(1100)	(1085)

Ratios are more meaningful

It should be appreciated that if there is a significant difference in turnover from what was forecast, a direct comparison of 'actual' balance-sheet figures with those budgeted, particularly in the case of working-capital items, will become increasingly less meaningful as the year progresses. Assessing performance in balance-sheet terms should, therefore, centre on the stability, or otherwise, of ratios. However, at least every quarter, the management accounts should have attached to them the financial manager's updated estimate of the year-end balance sheet, together with his comments on the amounts and causes for the expected changes.

All operating aspects of the management accounts should, either at separately convened meetings or collectively, be reviewed with the divisional or departmental managers. It is insufficient for the accounts just to be passed to the accountable managers — psychologically, much is to be gained from managers having to justify their results before their colleagues. The same applies at board meetings, where the directors, in their capacity as divisional managers, should be called upon to account.

Scrutinising the results

The item on the board agenda — 'monthly review of the management accounts' — should not be skimped either for want of time or because a cursory inspection of the figures indicates that they 'seem all right'. The finances of a company are the collective responsibility of all the directors, not just the financial director.

Use of ratios

Because many of the changed circumstances the financial manager finds himself facing are, to quite a large extent, self-compensating (a change in sales level, for example, would generally produce relative changes in stock, cash, debtors and creditors), ratios play a major part in the control function. In most balance-sheet respects the ratios are more relevant than the absolute figures. (The latter are of greater importance in relation to operating budgets and certain liquidity limits, such as bank facilities.)

In Chapter 3, reference was made to monitoring the six 'essential ratios' as being one of the best means for controlling working capital and, thereby, the day-to-day liquidity aspects of a company. These six ratios are regarded as the minimum requirement; most managers add liberally to the list depending upon the particularly significant factors in their own companies. For example, overheads, both in total and for specific items or groups, can usefully be related periodically to turnover, to factory output and to profits.

Some companies find it useful, particularly when comparing performance with other companies in the same group, to relate output, or sales or profits 'per man employed', per £1 of capital employed or per square foot of factory space. Only such statistics as can be shown to have use, and not just interest, should be produced.

Types of ratios

Ratios fall into two broad types:

1 Financial ratios — ones which involve items only found on the balance sheet; these are useful not only to financial managers, but to creditors and to shareholders
2 Operational ratios (sometimes called 'efficiency ratios') — ones which involve at least one item from the manufacturing, trading or profit and loss accounts; these are used almost exclusively by the financial manager and the divisional managers directly concerned

Of the six 'essential ratios', the current ratio and the quick ratio fall into the first category, while the last four are operational ratios. The stock ratio, the debtors ratio and the trade creditors ratio each relate an item on the balance sheet to an item on the operational accounts; the sixth one, the profit ratio, relates items which are both on these accounts.

Changes must be investigated

Changes in ratios, whether apparently for the better or worse, should always be fully investigated. Such changes should be regarded only as clues, not answers in themselves. This is particularly so in relation to liquidity management. For example, a rise in the current ratio might at first sight appear favourable, but could be due to a build-up of slow-moving stock. Similarly, a sale of goods on credit will transfer the items (at cost price) out of stock and (at selling price) into debtors. This fact alone will change, favourably, both the current ratio and the quick ratio, though if the debtor is likely to be a slow payer, the sale itself will neither help towards solving an immediate cash crisis, nor placate a pressing bank manager.

The six 'essential ratios'

The following statistics should be compiled by the financial manager monthly, and will provide the data on which to calculate the six principal ratios and such others as are relevant to the business:

Working capital

1 Stocks of:
  (*a*) Raw materials
  (*b*) Work-in-progress
  (*c*) Finished goods, appropriately broken down into main products
2 Debtors (divided into home and overseas customers):
  (*a*) Total amount due
  (*b*) Provision for doubtful debts
  (*c*) Amounts moderately overdue (totals, for, say, 1, 2 and 3 months overdue)
  (*d*) Amounts long overdue (individual items over £*X* with notes of action taken against each)
3 Cash and other current assets
4 Bank overdraft and other short-term financial liabilities (eg bills of exchange)
5 Trade and expense creditors:
  (*a*) Total amount for each
  (*b*) Amounts overdue and under query
6 Other current liabilities and their due dates:
  (*a*) Taxation
  (*b*) Dividends

Turnover

Appropriately broken down into main products.

Profit margins

1 Gross margins appropriately segregated into factories, processes, sales of products etc
2 Fixed overheads
3 Variable overheads
4 Net margins

Recording the ratios

The results of calculating the six principal ratios should be recorded in such a way as to show together the figures for years rather than months — it is the underlying trends, rather than any one month's ratios, which are of prime importance. Accordingly, such records would show as a minimum, probably in columnar form, the following:

Current ratio

1 Current assets

(*a*) MAT at beginning of month
(*b*) Total for month (added)
(*c*) Total for same month a year earlier (deducted)
(*d*) MAT at end of month

2 Current liabilities:
(*a*)-(*d*) as above

3 Month-end ratios (comparing 1 (*b*) with 2 (*b*))

4 MAT ratio which provides the weighted average ratio of the last 12 months (comparing 1 (*d*) with 2 (*d*))

Quick ratio
As for the current ratio but only quick assets included in the total 1. (An example of this type of record is given in the next section of this chapter.)

Stock ratio
1 Turnover (possibly also orders in hand):
(*a*) Total sales
(*b*) Sales by appropriate main products
Maintain each in monthly and MAT running totals as for the current ratio

2 Stocks:
(*a*) Total
(*b*) Finished goods by main products
Maintain each in monthly and MAT running totals

3 MAT ratio as for the current ratio. (In non-seasonal trades it is sometimes more meaningful to maintain three- or six-month running totals in preference to annual ones)

Debtors ratio
Number of days' sales represented by most recent sales (including VAT). Maintain monthly and MAT running totals.

Trade creditors ratio
Similar to debtors ratio. (Expense creditors due and overdue for payment can usefully be noted in total.)

Profit ratio
1 Sales
2 Cost of sales
3 Gross profit

Maintain each in total and for main products. Maintain each in monthly and MAT running totals as for the current ratio. As appropriate, maintain similar schedules of overheads, net profits etc.

Interpreting the ratios

The compiling of ratios, as with other financial data, will be to little effect if the results are not interpreted and such action as may be necessary is not initiated. It generally falls to the financial director, in making his monthly report to the board, to provide his interpretation of the causes of any changes; he may, if appropriate, also include his recommendations for the action to be taken to rectify any adverse trends.

A change in any ratio, as has already been stated, should be fully investigated, and it is assumed that this step would be carried out by the financial director before making his report.

Improving the ratios

The general conclusions to be deduced from the six principal ratios were commented upon in Chapter 3, together with a note on certain generally accepted norms (current ratio 1.5:1 and quick ratio 1.0:1). Clearly, it is in every company's interest to minimise the number of months' stock carried and the number of days' credit given to customers; conversely, the number of days' credit taken from suppliers should be maximised within reason. Profit margins should also be maximised within the limits imposed by both remaining competitive and complying with any prices legislation.

The first principles of any review of such ratios should be to see whether, if there has been movement, it has been in the favourable direction and, if not, the reasons for the adverse shift and whether it is likely to prove more than temporary. Comparisons with the budgeted plan should also be made, though, for example in the case of the debtors ratio, mere compliance with the forecast ratio, in this example the number of days' credit to be permitted, should not be taken as inhibiting the endeavours of the credit controller to better that forecast.

Use of graphs

The graphical presentation of certain financial data is strongly recommended not only for the financially untrained, but for the financial management as a whole. Few people have the ability to view a column of fluctuating results or statistics and to deduce mentally from them the underlying trends. And it is, very largely, the control of these trends which is at the heart of financial management. In highly seasonal businesses, where every month carries its own unique features, annual trends in particular provide the first clues to a company's fortunes, whether for the better or worse.

Simple line graphs

Bar charts are favoured by some managers, but experience of presenting financial data to widely differing company boards of directors shows that there is much to be said for appropriate results being supported by simple line graphs. These are generally maintained in the finance division, perhaps being made available on a side table in the boardroom at each monthly meeting. (One boardroom, known to the author, contains more than 50 graphs, all framed and affixed to the walls. As appropriate, each is made up daily, weekly or monthly and is always there for any manager to make a visual study of his division's or the company's performance.)

Like all internal statistics, records and ratios, only those which can provide useful information (or clues for further investigation) should be maintained.

Figure 13:2 gives an example (for a company with a seasonal trading pattern) of a less useful type of graph, but one which is commonly 'looked at'; it is not 'studied' because it tells the reader little that is not readily available from the monthly management accounts.

The monthly 'actual' line for the value of orders taken leaves the reader in doubt about whether the achievement is acceptable, bad or better than expected — similarly there is doubt about the significance of the 'year-to-date' line. Inclusion of lines depicting the 'budget to date' would help, but for selling purposes the corporate plan is really the determining factor as regards cumulative figures, not the financial year. MAT figures would, similarly, suffer from the underlying anachronism that each would, in part, be based on current data and in part on results which were quite irrelevant, being from a former and now either fulfilled or failed corporate plan.

Figure 13:3 sets out the same company's data, this time confined to the 12 months of the current corporate plan. Though the graph depicts the cumulative position, actual against budget, visually the emphasis is on the gap between objective and attainment.

Figure 13:2 Graph of orders taken (Unhelpful form)

	£'000		£'000
Actual		Year to date	3600
Month 1	1000	Month 7	900
Year to date	1000	Year to date	4500
Month 2	900	Month 8	1200
Year to date	1900	Year to date	5700
Month 3	800	Month 9	2400
Year to date	2700	Year to date	8100
Month 4	300	Month 10	2500
Year to date	3000	Year to date	10600
Month 5	200	Month 11	2000
Year to date	3200	Year to date	12600
Month 6	400	Month 12	900
Year to date	3600	Total for financial year	13500

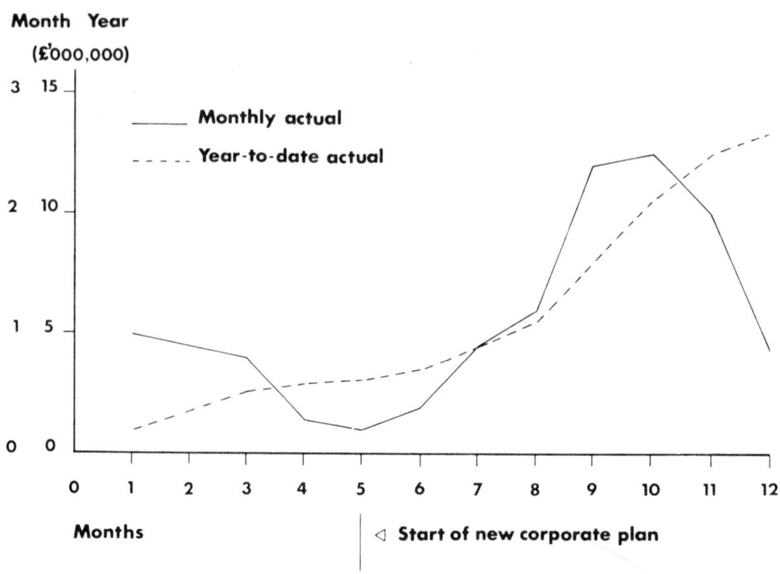

Figure 13:3 Graph of orders taken (Helpful form)

	Actual £'000	Budget £'000		Actual £'000	Budget £'000
			Year to date	9900	10500
Month 5	900	600	Month 11	1200	1000
Year to date	900	600	Year to date	11100	11500
Month 6	1200	1200	Month 12		1000
Year to date	2100	1800	Year to date		12500
Month 7	2400	2600	Month 1		1000
Year to date	4500	4400	Year to date		13500
Month 8	2500	2600	Month 2		500
Year to date	7000	7000	Year to date		14000
Month 9	2000	2200	Month 3		500
Year to date	9000	9200	Year to date		14500
Month 10	900	1300	Month 4		500
Year to date	9900	10500	Total for Marketing Year:		15000

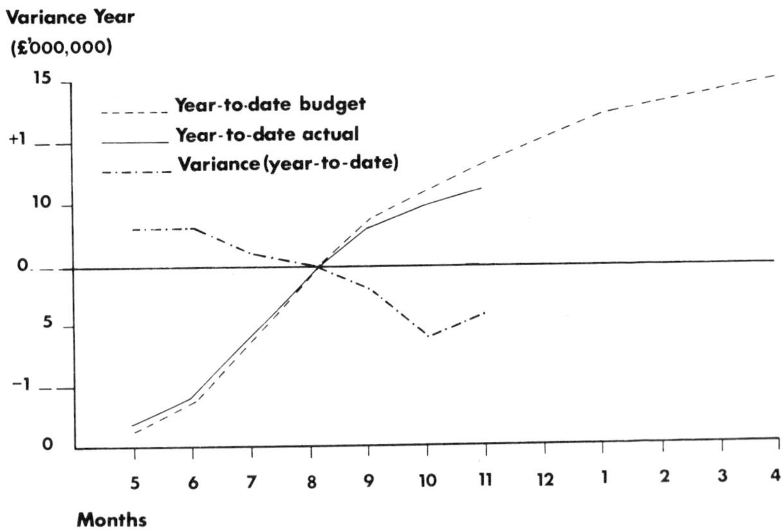

Figure 13:4 Graph of the trend in the quick ratio

	Quick assets £'000	Current liabilities £'000	Ratios Month	MAT
MAT	30,000	39,000		0.77
Month 6	+1,800	+3,600	0.50	
	-900	-2,300		
MAT	30,900	40,300		0.77
Month 7	+2,600	+3,600	0.72	
	-1,200	-2,800		
MAT	32,300	41,100		0.79
Month 8	+3,400	+4,000	0.85	
	-2,000	-3,500		
MAT	33,700	41,600		0.81
Month 9	+4,000	+4,000	1,00	
	-2,500	-3,400		
MAT	35,200	42,200		0.83
Month 10	+5,000	+4,100	1.22	
	-3,200	-2,800		
MAT	37,000	43,500		0.85

(Part only of the year's figures are shown)

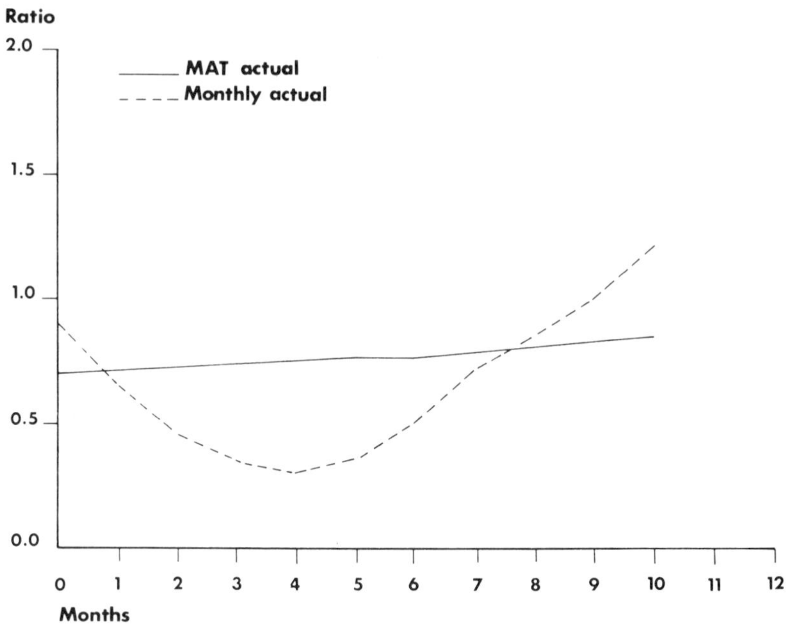

Balance-sheet graphs
In monitoring balance-sheet changes with the use of ratios, however, there is much to be said for maintaining MAT figures and for these to be presented graphically. Changes in balance-sheet ratios, except as a result of occasional major innovations such as the issue of new shares, happen relatively slowly and are not necessarily affected by increases or decreases in the level of sales.

Figure 13:4 gives an example of a highly seasonal company's quick ratio. When this ratio is calculated on just the month-end figures it varies very dramatically as stocks are built up (largely on suppliers' credit and short-term borrowings) before the main sales season is reached. Even if the monthly figures are compared with either the year before or with the monthly budgets, they will fail to show the underlying trend. This, it is suggested, can most easily be discerned from plotting the MAT of the ratios which, in the case illustrated, shows a slow, but steady, upward trend towards the generally accepted target of 1.0:1. (In practice, such MAT graphs should, whenever possible, allow for two years' movements to be plotted, thus even at the beginning of a year, the reader can see a minimum of 12 months' trend.)

It should be realised that the MATs of the quick assets and current liabilities are meaningless totals in themselves, and are of no value except when related to one another. (Note: Arithmetically, it is incorrect to try to 'shortcut' the calculation by taking an average of the 12 most recent individual monthly ratios.)

Age analysis of balances

Once a month the debtors balances on the sales ledger and the creditors balances on the bought and expenses ledgers should be extracted and analysed. Both such analyses should be prepared on a time basis, with each balance being broken down over the months it has accrued. In an effort to save time, some companies merely place each debt, in total, in the column indicated by the longest overdue part; this, it is suggested, has little value, especially when such oldest parts may be both trivial and have arisen just from errors in, say, calculating discounts.

An example of a creditors analysis is given in Figure 13:5. A debtors analysis would, in practice, need more columns, but would not show the discounts customers might claim.

If the invoices are prepared by, and ledgers kept on, a computer, by-products will include automatic ageing of debts and much useful sales statistics.

Figure 13:5 Age analysis of liabilities

Balances as at: 31 August

Supplier	May	June	July	August	Total	Discount*	Remarks
	£	£	£	£	£	£	
ABC Ltd			200	815	1015	15 (20 Sep)	
DEF Ltd		200	200		400		Price in dispute
GHI Ltd	675			5000	5675		Cr note awaited

*This column shows the amount of discount which could be claimed if payment were made by the date indicated

Controlling the contingency reserves

In Chapter 7 it was suggested that budgets should incorporate both (*a*) a general contingency reserve and (*b*) specific contingency reserves against specified headings where the extent of the expected cost could not, at the time of drawing up the budgets, be determined with accuracy.

A simple procedure is required for handling legitimate claims on these reserves, but it is essential that both types be adequately controlled by the authority which approved the original corporate plan and current year's budgets — the board of directors. Because they should not become involved with minor changes, it was stated earlier that specific reserves should only be created for 'unknowns' of significant size.

It is suggested that since the financial manager (or budget officer) is likely to be in frequent discussion with the operational managers, it is in conjunction with his monthly management accounts that requests should be submitted:

1 To receive an allocation from the general reserve on account of a complete set of new local circumstances (a general change of circumstances would probably warrant the preparation of new budgets generally), or
2 To take up a specified amount from the specific reserve as a result of an unknown factor (such as a major union wages claim) becoming quantifiable, or
3 To make any other alteration to the budgets after their approval (see Chapter 7)

The financial manager would then include these in his monthly financial report, perhaps commenting upon any particular significance in relation to the expected final results. Having approved such requisitions, the appropriate budgets for the remaining months would be adjusted. In this way, as far as is possible, 'like is compared with like' and the budget objectives remain reasonable in the manager's eyes. It is a more effective method than doing what many companies do, namely to add copious footnotes to the accounts sheets to the effect that 'so much' of a named variance on the accountable costs is of an 'uncontrollable' nature.

But whatever method is chosen, it is important for morale that managers should never be held accountable for 'non-controllable' variances even on 'controllable' items.

14

Signs of impending insolvency

The most sophisticated liquidity-management systems, even when really conscientiously applied, cannot guarantee survival. There is still much which can go sufficiently wrong to bring down an apparently successful business.

For example, the level of sales activity needed to maintain adequate profits may, quite suddenly, disappear. Losses can often be absorbed in the short term, but few companies have the resources to survive for long in other than profitable conditions — particularly during times of high inflation.

Economic conditions, or rather the public's awareness of them, can change very rapidly and virtually dry up whole markets; this is especially so in the luxury trades, which can also be affected overnight by the Chancellor's Budget changes (as happened with the boat-building industry in the wake of the imposition in 1975 of the 25 per cent VAT rate). Most companies guard against such eventualities to some extent; they can aim to serve as wide a market as possible at home and can try to establish a spread of overseas customers.

Customers and suppliers

Several highly successful small companies have failed because they relied too heavily on one or two customers who either failed or decided, in future, to produce such supplies themselves. Dependence upon a few customers is an undoubted threat to any business.

Dependence upon one or two suppliers also presents an undoubted threat. The supplying company can fail, it can be taken over by a competitor, or it may raise its prices unrealistically. Even at the cost of not obtaining quite such attractive terms from buying in bulk, it can be prudent in the long term to spread the company's custom over several competing suppliers.

Survival, therefore, is not only a questions of seeing that one's own company maintains its finances in good order. It is a matter of ensuring that the company's main suppliers and main customers are also maintaining their ability to survive. Liquidity-management techniques should ensure that any deterioration in the company's own financial position is quickly spotted. But how does a company detect impending troubles in other companies?

Judging the health of other companies

Published accounts at Companies House are of some help, but are usually a year or more out of date (if the company senses trouble it will most likely delay filing its accounts) and will only show the position at one date in the year which, if it has been so chosen, will reveal the best point in the company's seasonal cycle. Bank references are also of little practical value, though sometimes it is possible to read between the lines if the bank manager is spoken to (written replies tend to be couched in terms aimed primarily at defending their senders against any possible claims for libel). Dun and Bradstreet offer useful data to subscribers, as do certain other trade associations.

But much, it is suggested, can be learned about how other businesses are coping by the enquiring company's own staff. They should be alerted to look for and report upon the all too easily overlooked early-warning signs — the shabby vehicles and properties, the reduction in reception staff etc; competitors' staff can sometimes be met, their activities can possibly be monitored, any losses of agencies or franchises should be reported. There is much to be learned well short of embarking on the risky and unlawful paths of industrial espionage.

Insufficient capital

A very high proportion of companies which do not survive financially, fail for an insufficiency of capital relative to their level of activity. At the small-company level, if the proprietors lack adequate capital at the outset they will have no reserves with which to meet either emergencies or, in these days, the inevitable extra annual requirements on account of inflation.

Frequently, too great a part of what capital is available is locked up in fixed assets, more or less leaving the working-capital requirement to be sorted out by the local bank manager. Even if the bank does oblige, the overdependence on such short-term finance, which can be called in so suddenly, places the company in a permanently vulnerable position.

The extent of the net worth of another company, its permanent capital base, can be found from studying its published accounts. These will also show the extent to which any of its capital employed is surplus to its fixed assets. It is possible to calculate its financial ratios, but not all of its operational ratios (as defined in the previous chapter). A study of these ratios over several years may indicate an underlying trend. But, as has been stated, such information is only available as at one date in the year; furthermore, the published figures may give no indication of any trading losses which may have been incurred subsequently, and which would have eroded at least a part of the company's capital base.

Bad management

Probably the single most common root cause of business failure is the absence of good management; men of the calibre, and with the vision and astuteness, to see a company through the technological changes, the challenges and the pressures of 20th-century trading. Bad management can bring an otherwise good company down just as assuredly as the injection of first-class new management can turn round a poorly performing business. Its directors and managers should be amongst a company's most valued assets; alas, it would be more apt to rank the managements of some companies amongst their undisclosed liabilities.

Levels of staff turnover are generally a good guide to the competence of the management above. On the whole, 'founders' do not make good managers for it seems to be out of character for them to delegate; they therefore tend to collect weak managers about them. First-class technical managers, also, seldom make good general managers, and likewise talented creative types, for they often fail to appreciate the value and the need for both (*a*) team leadership and (*b*) administrative disciplines.

Accident-prone

In an article which appeared in *The Director* (September 1975), Mr John Argenti said:

> We cannot expect to forecast failure if we merely look for signs of financial deterioration. This deterioration occurs towards only the end of the process of failure. We might be better advised to direct our search to where the process starts... The earliest and clearest signs are almost certainly not financial, they are managerial, and

> they can be seen long before — perhaps years before — the company's financial position begins to deteriorate.

Mr Argenti goes on to suggest that companies appear to move through three stages on the way to failure:

1 They are defective in their top-management structure, in the way they respond to changes and in their accounting information systems (budgetary control, cash-flow planning and costing). These companies are accident-prone
2 Sooner or later, they make one or more fateful decisions, which lead ultimately to collapse and failure. They either overtrade, over-gear or they launch too large a project
3 The company's financial position then begins to show signs of obvious deterioration as does customer service. The maintenance of assets is postponed and so on

Mr Argenti concludes his description of this stage by saying:

> The company's financial reserves might allow it to fight a powerful rearguard action against the disaster facing it, thus prolonging the third stage for a number of years. Finally, in the last few months before insolvency, the company will search desperately for any source of capital at any price.

Accounting muddles

A fairly reliable guide that a supplier is, at best, badly managed and, at worst, in acute financial difficulties is given by the invoices and statements it sends out. If these are perpetually late, almost always seem to contain errors and credit notes are slow in being issued, the purchasing company has good cause for doubting that supplier's ability to survive. For if a company cannot get its sales ledger up to date and correct, the system it most depends upon for its cash receipts, it is fairly safe to assume its whole accounts department is in a mess; from this follows the almost equally safe assumption that the management is running the company 'blind', that there is precious little worthwhile budgeting and cash planning, and its failure is only a matter of time.

Occasionally an otherwise sound and well-run business is found being let down by its accounts department. But as a general rule, if a company's accounts department is in a mess then the whole company is in a mess also.

Avoiding liquidity crises

Undeniably, liquidity is the lifeblood of every business. It has been the aim of this book, not only to emphasise the need to plan and generally look after this unique and indispensable commodity — cash — but to descibe the practical steps which are necessary to avoid an unexpected crisis suddenly striking an unsuspecting management.

The recommended course of action to be followed by those managements who feel able to tackle the problem without outside professional help, can be summarised as follows:

1 Establish the options the company has for raising new funds and, most importantly, for improving the deployment of all existing resources (Part 3)
2 Plan every aspect of the business programme in financial terms such that the cash-flow projections are an integral part of this programme (Part 4)
3 Monitor the results achieved and initiate such action as may be necessary at the first signs of the financial position deteriorating, in order to bring the company back on to its planned course (Part 5).

Index